THE LORDSHIP OF CHRIST

The Expression and Witness of Jesus Christ's Authority over Every Believer

MARK D. MICHAEL

ISBN 979-8-88751-909-8 (paperback)
ISBN 979-8-88751-910-4 (digital)

Christian Faith Publishing
832 Park Avenue
Meadville, PA 16335
www.christianfaithpublishing.com

All biblical citations were taken from the King James Version of the Holy Bible unless otherwise indicated.

Printed in the United States of America

CONTENTS

CHAPTER 1

The Way Up Is Down

Most believers have heard someone say, "Jesus is Lord!" It is a commonly used statement among Christians. It is also a true statement, but what does it mean? The purpose of this book is to research the meaning and significance of lordship. Jesus Christ is our Lord today, but he was not always Lord. Many saints fail to understand and appreciate the fact that *Lord* is a title that Jesus won. Consider the uniqueness of a verse like Acts 2:36 (KJV)., which states, "Therefore let all the house of Israel know assuredly, that God has made that same Jesus, whom ye have crucified both Lord and Christ." It is a declaration of an accomplishment! The biblical testimony says that Jesus existed with God from the beginning. "In the beginning was the Word, and the Word was with God, and the Word was God. The same was in the beginning with God" (John 1:1–2). In this scripture, the person we know today as Jesus is identified as being "the Word." John removes any doubt that Jesus and "the Word" are one and the same by writing, "And the Word was made flesh and dwelt among us, and we beheld his glory, the glory as of the only begotten of the Father, full of grace and truth" (John 1:14). This establishes Jesus as preincarnate, meaning he existed as God before he was born as a person into this world. Philippians corroborates his preincarnation, saying of Jesus that before the world was created, he was both "in the form of God" and "thought it not robbery to be equal with God" (Philippians 2:6). This confirms that before all things were created, there existed God the Father and "the Word," whom we know today as Jesus Christ. Jesus was always there, and he was always God. But he was not always Lord, and he was not always God's Son. As I have already stated, before creation, Jesus existed in the form of God. He was of the same substance and material as the Father. Yet there was something about Jesus that was different, something that made him special to the Father. Philippians 2:6 says that although he was in the form of God, he did not consider the status of being God as something to be held on to (paraphrase). This simply means that equality with God was not Jesus's desire. Instead of focusing on the status of being equal with Father God, he instead deeply desired to please the Father. Because of Jesus's humility, the Father determined to glorify him, make him his Son, and give him a kingdom of people who would call him their Lord.

Before creation, the Father and the Word conspired together. The conspiracy went something like this: Jesus would come to earth and become a man. He would be firstly, God's only begotten Son, born of a woman. Secondly, he would redeem mankind back to God. Thirdly, the Father would exalt and elevate his human form, Son, before men and make him Lord of all creation. In turn, as all creation would honor and praise Jesus as the Son of God, Jesus would then glorify the Father by submitting himself and his glory back to the Father. As God's Son would be glorified by men and angels, so the Father would be glorified also. We can see this divine conspiracy reported on and played out in scripture. In the process of time, the Virgin Mary was notified that she was chosen to be a part of the divine plan, and the first step of her being impregnated was completed (Luke 1:26–31). This act of God impregnating Mary is often referred to as the Immaculate Conception. The biblical account of this event reports,

> And the angel said unto her, Fear not, Mary: for
> thou hast found favor with God. And behold,
> thou shalt conceive in thy womb and bring forth
> a son, and shalt call his name JESUS. He shall be

great, and shall be called the Son of Highest: and
the Lord God shall give him the throne of his
father David. (Luke 1:30–32)

With Mary's impregnation, the Word had become flesh, and according to the Holy Spirit's command, men began to call him by the name Jesus. While this scripture testifies of the virgin birth, there are other scriptures that testify of the conspiracy. Speaking from his preincarnate voice, Jesus announces the purpose of his coming, saying, "Then said I, Lo I come (in the volume of the book it is written of me) to do thy will, O God" (Hebrews 10:7). Jesus was elevated to Lord because he was willing to submit himself to the Father, become a mere man, and die on the cross. His becoming man would not be a temporary matter. Jesus would be permanently both God and man. God the Father fashioned Jesus and formed a body for him so that he could become Mary's child—a man. "And being found in fashion as a man, he humbled himself" (Philippians 2:8). God then placed the recreated Jesus into Mary's womb. Thus, Jesus, who had been "the Word" and in the very form of God, became a human baby in the form of a man.

The next confirmation of this divine conspiracy was the official announcement that Jesus had become God's Son. God had spoken to Mary before her inception and announced that the baby she would birth would be the Son of God. But God did not leave this revelation to just Mary's testimony. God personally testified about the origin of Jesus himself on several occasions. "And lo a voice from heaven, saying, 'This is my beloved Son, in whom I am well pleased'" (Matthew 3:17). In this divine drama, the Father was not conspiring alone. Jesus was coconspirator in this plan. Jesus knew that if he suffered and redeemed fallen humanity, he would be rewarded with the title of Lord of all those he would redeem. Romans 14:9 says, "For to this end Christ both died, and rose, and revived, that he might be Lord of all." This word *might* implies "potential." The first part of the divine conspiracy was that through Mary, Jesus would become God's Son. The second part of the divine conspiracy was that after Jesus's suffering, death, and resurrection, he would be elevated to lordship, and the Father would be glorified through his Son. All who call Jesus Lord, and all who submit to him as their Lord would bring glory to the Father. After all the planning was ratified in heaven, God called it done before Jesus even descended to the earth. The Father declared that all men would worship his Son, the Lord Jesus, who was "slain from the foundation of the world" (Revelation 13:8).

Sometime after the divine conspiracy was ratified, the Father and the Word began creation. Speaking of Jesus in his preincarnate status as the Word, Colossians 1:16 says, "For by him were all things created, that are in heaven, and that are in earth, visible and invisible…all things were created by him, and for him." Speaking also of creation, John 1:3 says, "All things were made by him and without him was not anything made that was made." These scriptures declare that all things were created by Jesus. This, therefore, gave him the right to be Lord over all things. This matter of being the divine host of all creation was a precursor to his being Lord. After creation, God began to call men to salvation at first through a nation of people called Israel and then through reapers called to preach the gospel and bring in God's harvest. A great while after the creation, Apostle Paul came to us, implementing the divine program. In Romans 10:9, Paul writes, "That if thou shalt confess with thy mouth the Lord Jesus, and shalt believe in thine heart that God hath raised him from the dead, thou shalt be saved." This is the genesis of the divine conspiracy. The rest of this book is written to help you understand the process by which Jesus became Lord and the significance his lordship to you as a believer.

Jesus's Humility

The person Jesus, being formerly the Word, had assisted the Father in creating all things. But after creation, the created man, Adam, sinned in the garden. God's created man had fallen and was eternally separated from God. Jesus knew the deep love the Father had for his creation. Because pleasing the Father was his ultimate focus and goal, Jesus came down into the earth to redeem God's creation. Jesus's goal in coming into the earth was expressly to do God's will.

As I stated previously, what made Jesus special to the Father was his great humility. Apostle Paul, as he exhorts the Philippians, encourages them to be like Jesus. They are to have "lowliness of mind," and they are to "esteem others better than themselves" (Philippians 2:3). These are the characteristics of Jesus and the characteristics of his followers. Paul goes on to describe Jesus's great humility. In three different ways, Jesus humbled himself, each being a more profound humiliation than the former. Philippians 2:7 says that he "made himself of no reputation and took upon him the form of a servant." Jesus did not come to earth as a great earthly king, but as a foot-washing servant of men. Philippians 2:7 also says that he "was made in the likeness of man." It took great humility for Jesus to lay aside his status as the Word, divine, and be made into merely a mortal man. Even after becoming a man, his humiliation was not complete. He would have to submit to death by crucifixion. Philippians 2:8 says that he "became obedient unto death, even the death of the cross." These are three levels of humility Jesus exercised in coming to earth and doing God's will. From his heavenly status of being God, Jesus did not take a partial humility and become an angel, or perhaps even an archangel. Instead, he took upon himself the nature and existence of a mortal man. There was no place in him for pseudo-humility. Even as a man, he did not come to earth as an earthly king or an honored human being. He came to us as a street-walking, foot-washing servant. These are the first two levels of humiliation. Jesus was found and fashioned as a man. He did this simply because it pleased the Father. Finally, after he had made himself lower than any angel in heaven, after he had made himself a servant even to men, after men had spat on him and ridiculed him and beat him during the process of his crucifixion, Jesus was still not humbled fully. From the cross at Golgotha, as he struggled with the load of the sins of the world, he had one more task to complete. He had to humble himself to die. Can you understand the gravity of this matter? God was on that cross trying to learn how to die. God is not the author of death; he is the author of life. There is no death in heaven—only life. It took great humility for Jesus to submit himself to death, but he did it for you and me.

Christ's Elevation

The next verse in Philippians 2:9 begins with the word *wherefore*. "Wherefore God also hath highly exalted him, and given him a name which is above every name" (Philippians 2:9). In this verse, the word "wherefore" simply means "for this reason." Because of Jesus's humility, because he was willing to diminish himself to abject obscurity, God granted Jesus promotion. After his humiliation and suffering, and upon his resurrection, God was so pleased with Jesus that he promoted him to the heavenly office of being *Lord*. The Bible does not just say that God has exalted him; it says that God has "highly exalted him" (Philippians 2:9). The heavenly Father made a royal decree that his Son, Jesus, was now Lord to both men and angels. Today, Jesus is Lord of all. Because he has been exalted, the status of his name has also changed. God has "given him a name which is above every name" (Philippians 2:9). The elevation of Jesus is expressed in his name. If Jesus is Lord of all, then all must submit to his name. But we must understand that Jesus is not just Lord of men on earth; he is also Lord in heaven, and he is also Lord in hell. "That at the name of Jesus every knee should bow, of things in heaven, and things in earth, and things under the earth" (Philippians 2:10). And not only shall all bow to Jesus Christ; all men must also confess that he is Lord. "And that every tongue should confess that Jesus Christ is Lord, to the glory of God the Father" (Philippians 2:11). This scripture is the very first principle and first point of order for the Christian faith. God making Jesus Lord is the doorway to salvation. There is no other door. To every man who agrees with Jesus being their Lord and confesses the same, God grants the benefit of salvation. Every man who resists this decree, ignores this decree, or rebels against this decree is in direct opposition to God. Every man who confesses that Jesus is Lord not only agrees with God's decree, but he also glorifies God. Romans 14:11 is a first-person declaration from the Lord Jesus! "For it is written, as I live, saith the Lord, every knee shall bow to me, and every tongue shall confess to God." Thus, as I have stated, Romans 10:9 becomes a type of "doorway" into the faith. It is the doorway into the salvation experience. "That if thou shalt confess with thy mouth the Lord Jesus, and shalt believe in thine heart that God hath raised him from the dead, thou shalt be saved" (Romans 10:9). Notice that Romans 10:9 does not mention the word *savior*. There is no mention of the word *savior* because saving men is an act, but Lord is a rank. Lord is who Jesus is, and saving men is what he does. He can only be your Savior as a result of his being your Lord. If he is not your Lord, then he is not your Savior.

"Son of God" and "Son of Man"

If you have understood all that I have said thus far, then you realize that Jesus Christ is both God and man. When Jesus walked the earth, he made two references to himself. He referred to himself as the "Son of God" and also as the "Son of man." The reference "the Son of man" is indicative of the fact that the divine had now become fully human—a man. The reference to "the Son of God" was indicative of the fact that Jesus, the man, was the divine offspring of God. He was God before all the worlds were created, and he became man by coming into our world through the virgin Mary. He is the Son of God by nature, and he is the Son of man by birth. God the Father bore witness of his Son. "And lo a voice from heaven, saying, This is my beloved Son, in whom I am well pleased" (Matthew 3:17). Thus, we can now refer to Jesus as the God-man.

As stated earlier, Jesus's first task in coming to earth was to glorify God before men. Jesus confirms this himself, saying, "I have glorified thee on the earth: I have finished the work which thou gave me to do. And now O Father, glorify thou me with thine own self with the glory which I had with thee before the world was" (John 17:4–5). In the divine drama, Jesus had a task he had to complete, and the Father did also. Jesus's task was to glorify the Father. The Father's task was to glorify the Son. Jesus would do his part by teaching men the ways of God and then by dying on the cross for their sins. Jesus declared the completion of his assignment. "When Jesus therefore had received the vinegar, he said, 'It is finished,' and he bowed his head, and gave up the ghost" (John 19:30). Thus, his work was complete. The Father had promised Jesus that if he completed the task he was assigned to do, he would be raised from the dead and glorified. The Father did his part by raising Jesus from the grave in a mighty resurrection. After the resurrection, the Father, seeing the work had been completed, and bringing Jesus back to his throne in heaven, said to his Son, Jesus, "Sit thou at my right hand, until I make thine enemies thy footstool" (Psalm 110:1). With these words, the Father began the work of glorifying his Son, a work that is still ongoing this day. Men are employed to assist the Father in the work of glorifying the Lord Jesus. Are you assisting the Father in this work?

What's in a Name?

The biblical nomenclature referencing the names of Jesus is also very important. Each of the biblical references to the person of Jesus are for the purpose of making the proper emphasis in our thinking. Jesus was born into the world as the man named Jesus. The angel says to Joseph, "And she shall bring forth a son, Thou shalt call his name Jesus" (Matthew 1:21). Thus, the name Jesus becomes the reference that emphasizes his humanity. The name Jesus designates him as a historical person and fully human. Those who also believe that this Jesus was sent by God to be his Messiah would then refer to him as Jesus Christ or Jesus the Christ or Jesus the Messiah or Jesus the Anointed One of God. To believe he is the Messiah or Christ is to believe that he was sent by Father God into the world to save men. You must believe not only in the historical person Jesus; you must believe he was sent by God to be his Christ. "Jesus saith unto them, But whom say ye that I am? And Simon Peter answered and said, 'Thou art the Christ, the Son of the living God'" (Matthew 16:15–16). Thus, the phrase *Jesus Christ* becomes the name designation that emphasizes his humanity in conjunction with his divinity. This is also called the hypostatic union. The hypostatic union is a theological term that references the combination of the divine and human natures in a single person called Christ. To say "Jesus Christ" is to reference both a historical human person who is also divine. After Jesus's resurrection, he is referred to as Christ Jesus. "There is therefore now no condemnation to them who are in Christ Jesus" (Romans 8:1).

This reference emphasizes the fact that he is fully divine and fully human. The term *Christ Jesus* also references the hypostatic union, but the emphasis here is on his divinity, the title Christ being placed first here for this emphasis. However, the highest biblical reference would be to simply use the term *Christ*. This term puts full emphasis on his divinity. It speaks of the glorified Lord who has returned to his high office and throne with all power. This reference omits his humanity and deliberately emphasizes his divinity only. This title is often referenced with many of the "in Christ" quotations of the New Testament. In addition to the reference Christ, we, as believers, also refer to him as Lord. The term *Lord* is personal. It is the proper term for those who recognize his rank and who are submitted to him. Therefore, in many of the New Testament references, the term *Christ* and *Lord* are used interchangeably. "Blessed be the God and Father of our Lord Jesus Christ, who hath blessed us with all spiritual blessings in heavenly places in Christ" (Ephesians 1:3, emphasis added). As you read the New Testament, pay close attention to which reference is being used and what the Holy Spirit is seeking to emphasize as he may use Jesus, Jesus Christ, Christ Jesus, Christ, or Lord.

"I Am the Lord"

The believer must come to realize that *Lord* is an authoritative title. When you say "Lord," you are speaking of the one who is in charge. Many modern minds cannot properly appreciate this. When the Bible uses the term *Lord*, it is referring to Christ's absolute authority and power over all his subjects. Jesus is Lord! We can see this matter quite clearly in some of the Old Testament passages. In many places in the Old Testament, God emphasizes his authority by using the phrase *I am the Lord* as a signature. The phrase *the Lord* comes from the transliteration of the Hebrew word *Jehovah*. What many saints fail to recognize is the implicit deeper authoritative demand behind the phrase *I am the Lord* or *I am Jehovah*. I want to share with you a few scriptures where the Lord is giving out his will and making commandments to Israel. When reading your Bible, never read the phrase *I am the Lord* casually. Instead, imagine an earthly father speaking sternly to his children as if he will not tolerate their disobedience. In scripture, this is no earthly father but instead the Almighty God. The following scriptures are Old Testament references. They are chosen here because of the reference to his lordship:

> Ye shall not eat anything with the blood: neither shall ye use enchantment, or observe the times. Ye shall not round the corners of your heads, neither shall you mar the corners of your beard. Ye shall not make cuttings in your flesh for the dead, nor print any marks upon you: **I am the Lord**. (Leviticus 19:26–28, emphasis added)

We can easily see that the refrain "I am the Lord" is an emphasis. Do not read it casually but hear the emphasis that the Lord is declaring. Let's look at another scripture where the Lord signs his name.

> Do not prostitute thy daughter, to cause her to be a whore; lest the land fall into whoredom, and the land become full of wickedness. Ye shall keep my Sabbaths and reverence my sanctuary: **I am the Lord**. (Leviticus 19:29–30, emphasis added)

As you read this, you should stop and ask yourself the question, Why does God periodically stop in the midst of his monologue and say, "I am the Lord?" He does this for emphasis. It is his way of authoritatively saying, "You will do as I say!" In Luke 6:46, Jesus is speaking to his disciples. He says, "And why call ye me Lord, Lord, and do not the things which I say?" The word *Lord* must have meaning to the believer. If saying the word *Lord* has no significance to you, your salvation is in jeopardy. Let us consider another scripture where this statement is used.

> And the slain shall fall in the midst of you, and ye shall know that **I am the Lord**… And they shall know that **I am the Lord**, and that I have not

said in vain that I would do this evil unto them.
(Ezekiel 6:7,10, emphasis added)

It is obvious here that when God writes "I am Jehovah" or "I am the Lord," it means something to him. Does it mean anything to you?

CHAPTER 2

Lordship Relationship: Submission and Obedience

The ninth chapter of the book of Acts opens with an exposé on a man named Saul. He was a Jewish man, zealous for the traditions of his forefathers. He was incensed with a group called Christians because they were of a different way, custom, or tradition from his own. In his religious fervor, he requested authority from the high priest to "bring them all bound in chains to Jerusalem" (Acts 9:1–2). His deep devotion to God and his love of the Jewish religion drove him. But as he journeyed to do his business, he came near a road called Damascus. Suddenly, there shined a light from heaven around about him, and he fell to the earth. His journey was supernaturally interrupted by the risen Lord Jesus Christ. We are able to learn something about lordship from Saul's experience and response to that powerful light. Saul's first response to the light was to declare, "Who art thou, Lord?" (Acts 9:5) Saul, without instruction, intuitively perceived that the one he was talking to was the Lord. Saul was not an earthly disciple of Jesus. Therefore, this reference to Lord was by perception. Saul perceived the divinity of the one who talked to him and intuitively called him Lord. Anytime you touch the risen Christ, you will perceive his lordship. Although Paul was correct in calling him Lord, Jesus still identified himself. Jesus introduced himself to Paul as a person. "I am Jesus, whom thou persecutes" (Acts 9:5). The Lord Jesus introduced himself to Saul that day and initiated a personal relationship to him. We can interpret this initial introductory step of "meeting the Lord" as the day Saul became "born-again." To be born again represents having a new relationship with the Lord Jesus. It is only after this "born-again" relationship begins that Saul's name is subsequently changed to Paul. All the production of Paul's ministry emanated from this born-again relationship. The recognition of Christ's lordship is initiated at the born-again experience, and that is where our relationship with Jesus must begin. That day, Saul met Jesus and became born-again, and he immediately began expressing lordship. Every believer must walk under lordship. Saul embraced lordship from the very beginning and carried that sense of lordship throughout his ministry. However, it is possible to acknowledge lordship in an initial sense and then allow that sense of lordship to fade and grow dull. This is the state of many believers. They are born-again but simultaneously estranged from their Lord. Lordship simply means accountability to Christ. The believer who is walking under lordship lives his life with an acute sense of being accountable to the Lord Jesus. On the other hand, a person who is simply a "Christian" is prescribing to a set of beliefs and values that are associated with the teachings of a historical person named Jesus. This is what separates the believer from the Christian.

Submission and Obedience

In order to walk in a lordship relationship with Jesus Christ, there must be submission and obedience. Submission is the act, or fact, of yielding to a superior. After Paul was introduced to the Lord Jesus on the Damascus Road, he asked Jesus a second question. "Trembling and astonished, he asked, 'Lord, what will thou have me to do?'" (Acts 9:6). Notice once again that he referred to him as Lord. Once we have a lordship relationship to Jesus, we are guided daily by an awareness of our accountability and a personal quest to stay in his will. "What do you want me to do, Lord?" becomes the mantra of our lives. The scripture says, "And that he died for all, that they which live should not henceforth live unto themselves, but unto him which died for them, and rose again" (2 Corinthians 5:15). Submission is a disposition. It is an attitude. Submission is living your life for the Lord, to do his will, and to walk in his ways. After meeting Jesus on the Damascus Road, Paul was no longer willing to live out his own agenda but instead to do whatever the Lord told him to do. This is lordship. Lordship is expressed through the believer's submission to the Lord. But after submission, there must be obedience. Obedience is compliance with an order, request, or law. Jesus was referencing obedience when he said, "Not everyone that saith unto me, Lord, Lord, shall enter into the kingdom of heaven; but he that doeth the will of my Father which is in heaven" (Matthew 7:21). After Paul showed submission, he asked what the Lord required of him. Once he receives a command, his obedience to the Lord would then be tested. The next phrase in the verse is, "And the Lord said" (Acts 9:6). Notice in the previous verse, Jesus says to Saul, "I am Jesus, whom thou persecute" (Acts 9:5). Yet in the very next verse, we see these words, "and the Lord said" (Acts 9:6). This is because Jesus is now Lord to Paul, and he speaks to him no more as Jesus but as his Lord. "And the Lord said unto him, Arise and go into the city, and it shall be told thee what thou must do" (Acts 9:6). Obedience means compliance to an order. It is going where the Lord tells you to go, doing what the Lord tells you to do, and submitting to whom the Lord tells you to submit to. This is the confident, faith-based relationship that you must develop with the Lord Jesus. As we submit to the Lord, others who are also in submission to him will often be called upon to instruct us. Submitting to the Lord also means submitting to his delegated authority. Those who say, "Only the Lord can tell me what to do" do not understand lordship. Paul was obedient to the Lord's instruction. Blinded on the Damascus Road, Paul journeyed without sight into Damascus to await his next instruction from whatever person the Lord delegated. This is lordship!

In Damascus, there was another believer named Ananias who also knew Jesus as his Lord. The Lord had appeared to Ananias in a vision. "And [Ananias] said, Behold, I am here Lord" (Acts 9:10). Notice Ananias refers to Jesus as his Lord. This is the lordship relationship at work.

> And the Lord said unto him, Arise, and go into
> the street which is called Straight and enquire in
> the house of Judas for one called Saul of Tarsus:
> for behold he prayeth. And hath seen in a vision
> a man named Ananias coming in and putting
> his hand on him that he might receive his sight.
> (Acts 9:11–12)

This command was disturbing to Ananias. He had heard many bad things about Saul, and he feared for his life (Acts 9:13–14). But the Lord said unto him, "Go thy way: for he is a chosen vessel unto me" (Acts 9:15). Although Ananias was in submission to the Lord, and the relationship was one of authority, yet it was not autocratic. Ananias freely expressed his fears to the Lord. "I have heard many things about this man" (Acts 9:13–14). The Lord offered him an explanation to console him, but still expected him to trust and be obedient despite his fears. Although the Lord is all-powerful and has complete control, he does not bully his people. This is the character of the Lord, and this is another example of the lordship relationship at work. You have seen how the Lord Jesus related to both Paul and Ananias. The lordship relationship is personal. Other believers will not know every assignment the Lord gives to you, as you will not know every assignment that the Lord gives them. The lordship relationship is a personal relationship, yet it demands submission and obedience.

> And Ananias went his way and entered into the
> house; and putting his hands on (Saul) said,
> Brother Saul, the Lord, even Jesus, that appeared
> unto thee in the way as thou camest, hath sent
> me, that thou might receive thy sight and be
> filled with the Holy Ghost. And immediately
> there fell from his eyes as it had been scales: and
> he received sight forthwith, and arose, and was
> baptized. (Acts 9:17–18)

Ananias referred to Jesus both by his earthly name Jesus and by his elevated title of being Lord. We should also note that Ananias's admonition was that it was the Lord's will that Paul be "filled with the Holy Ghost." The lordship life is the spirit-filled life. This is the will of the Lord for every believer. After a person is born again, there should follow both water baptism and the receiving of the baptism in the Holy Spirit.

Paul and Ananias became acquaintances that day by the will of the Lord. Lordship is not individualism; it is living your life with an awareness and regard for the body of Christ. When two believers meet, their common ground is the lordship of Jesus Christ. If two believers meet and one of them is not in submission to Jesus as his Lord, the two will not find a profound fellowship with one another. My wife and I have met believers in airports, foreign countries, vacation resorts, and the like, and if they are in submission to Jesus as their Lord, the Holy Spirit will begin a supernatural dialog that blesses us all. I do not mean that if two people are Christian, this will occur. I have met many people who were declared Christians but did not experience this. As you begin to develop a lordship relationship to Jesus, he is going to open up his kingdom to you. When this happens, everyone who calls Jesus Lord with meaning will take on a new significance to you. Not only will you be able to perceive what the will of the Lord is for your own life, but your relationship to other believers who are in submission to Jesus as their Lord will become vibrant and dynamic as well. This is lordship!

The Twenty-Year Veteran and the Rookie

I met my wife, Sandra, over ten years ago. When I met Sandra, I knew more Bible than she did. I also knew more church than she did. Sandra had been saved for only about six years. I had been saved and preaching the gospel for over twenty years. I was certainly born again, and I also had a healthy fear of the Lord. I respected and feared the fact that the Lord would one day judge me. But I did not have a proper lordship relationship with Jesus Christ. The Lord introduced Sandra to me, and he created a mentoring relationship between us.

But contrary to what you might expect, I was not mentoring Sandra; she was mentoring me. This happened for one specific reason. God wanted her to teach me how to relate to him as my Lord. That does not mean that I didn't say "Lord" in my daily talk or in sermons or in church. I said "Lord" often. But I did not truly know Christ as "my Lord" in a personally authoritative way. The primary difference between Sandra and me was that I had a biblical, somewhat intellectual, relationship to the Lord while Sandra had a personal and submitted relationship to the Lord. I was navigating my life based on biblical principles and standards for being a Christian. However, when Sandra came along, she began to speak to me explicitly about how the Lord spoke to her, corrected her, and guided her daily. When Sandra and I talked, my conversation was like, "These are the things we should be doing as Christians." Her conversation was more like, "This morning the Lord told me that he is moving on my behalf in this situation." My Christian walk was based on reading the instruction manual; Sandra's Christian walk was based on talking directly to the Instructor.

My knowledge of Scripture had not prohibited the enemy from hindering my life. I needed to learn another important step of acknowledgment and submission to the Lord Jesus. James 4:7 says, "Submit yourselves therefore to God. Resist the devil, and he will flee from you." Biblical principles are the standards we use to establish our Christian lives upon, but they are not a substitute for our relationship to the Lord Jesus. God wrote the Bible on the level where man, in his fallen state, could get a better understanding and appreciation for his ways and his will. When you write a note to your four-year-old, it is not a reflection of your full knowledge. Through my relationship with Sandra, the Lord began to expose all the areas where the enemy had put me in bondage despite my best biblical thinking. Our fallen intellect cannot substitute for the Lord's divine authority over our lives. Our intellect is inadequate to accomplish the will of God even if we have a few scriptures in there. Only submission to his lordship will suffice. It is not the quoting of our favorite scripture that will be efficacious for our deliverance. Our connection to a local church or pastor is good, but it should never be a substitute for lordship. It is only when the believer is walking under lordship that his life becomes pleasing to God.

Some believers have a better understanding and appreciation of lordship than others. If you have not had lordship taught to you or "modeled" for you by another believer, then you will have to learn lordship through divine mentoring. Some people were not necessarily taught about lordship; they instead observed someone who served Christ as their Lord. As a young Christian, I was taught about the cross and how Jesus died for my sins. I was also told that I had to "accept" Jesus as Lord to be saved. I also received some basic biblical and theological instruction. But these same believers who instructed me in being a Christian, too often had a weak sense of direct accountability to Jesus as their Lord. They did not teach or model a life of submission and obedience. These mentors too often had a poor sense of accountability to Jesus Christ in their personal life. They knew the Bible but not necessarily lordship!

You Must Die

When my wife and I were first married, we had a lot of disagreements and contentions between us in our marriage. It is important to know that being Christian does not mean your character has been perfected. One of the natural consequences of marital arguments is the conclusion that the other party is the one who is wrong. After one of our big arguments, we both agreed that we would seek the Lord about our marriage. We had a mutual friend who was a prophetess. She had spoken prophetically to both of us on several occasions. My wife and I both were convinced that she heard accurately from the Lord Jesus. We called this friend on the phone and told her our situation. She asked us to give her some time to seek the Lord about our marriage. She called us back a few days later and said, "The Lord told me that both of you will have to die!" Of course, she meant this metaphorically. Sandra and I both were taken aback. We both knew that the word of the Lord is true. When the Lord said, "You both must die," he was referring to the fact that the contentions we were experiencing in our marriage was the result of both our need to decrease. "You both must die" meant that in order for us to have a happy marriage, we both had to die to "self," "die to pride," "die to our personal agendas," "die to attitudes," "die to mentalities," and so forth. You cannot maintain marriage if you have not died.

I wanted to tell this story about my wife and I to draw out an important parallel. For a person to walk under lordship, he/she must die. The very concept of lordship is repugnant to you if you have not died to yourself. If Jesus is to be Lord over your life, you have to cease being "lord" over your own life. You must die. You must die to this world. You must die to your own ideas. You must die to your own fleshly perspective. You must die to your ways. You must die to your intellect. You must die to the devil. Only when there is only one Lord in your life will you see the manifestation of the kingdom of God. There are many scriptures that support this theory of death. Apostle Paul wrote, "I am crucified with Christ; nevertheless I live; yet not I but Christ liveth in me: and the life which I now live in the flesh, I live by the faith of the Son of God, who loved me and gave himself for me" (Galatians 2:20). This scripture emphasizes the fact that there is a "death" that is not associated with breathing. Jesus came into this world to die. We are never being more like our Lord than we are when we have died to the things of this world. We must come to understand this biblical principle that to reap life, we must sow death. When we die, we allow life to be birthed in our circumstance and in the circumstances of others around us. "So then death worketh in us but life in you" (2 Corinthians 4:12). Your prayer should be that the Lord will help you to die, so that he can truly become Lord over your life.

Dual Loyalties

After Paul's Damascus road experience, he renounced his devotion and affiliation to the men and institutions that had endorsed him and sent him to persecute Christians. He later renounced other cherished devotions in his life so that he could build upon his relationship with Jesus Christ. Paul declared, "But what things were gained to me, those I counted loss for Christ. Yea doubtless, and I count all things but loss for the excellency of the knowledge of Christ Jesus my Lord" (Philippians 3:7–8). He did not return to the high priest or to the Jewish leaders. His new devotion was to his Lord. The rest of Paul's life had the singular focus of love, admiration, and service to Christ. To walk under lordship means that you do not live your life by ideologies, affiliations, or earthly loyalties. To walk under the lordship of Christ is to have the singular commitment to pleasing the Lord. The lordship question that many believers must wrestle with is, what ideologies, people, groups, or institutions compete with you, having a stronger relationship with the Lord? Many believers' lives cannot truly reflect Christ because they have focused themselves on supporting the ideological agendas of this world. Their lives are like the back end of a car, filled with bumper stickers. The bumper stickers are political, ideological, environmental, and philosophical, and one or two of them may be religious. These believers erroneously believe that by being multifarious and eclectic in their interest, they are being more like God. But Christ did not call us to represent all of the ideals of this world. Christ has called us to represent and glorify him, and him alone. If Christ is not the only "bumper sticker" on your life, then he is not your Lord, and you are not glorifying him. Jesus said, "No man can serve two masters: for either he will hate the one, and love the other; or else he will hold to the one, and despise the other. Ye cannot serve God and mammon" (Matthew 6:24). Although this scripture is often used to teach about the love of money, we must not fail to see that what Jesus was also teaching about was the danger of dual loyalties. To try to serve God and mammon means that your heart is divided between the two. When the believer is trying to be loyal to more than one thing, he loses his influence. If your life is to please God, you must become single-minded in your perspective. In life, we may have many different interests. However, where these interests rank in our hearts and minds says much about whether we have made Jesus our Lord.

Jesus also taught this principle of dual loyalty in another way, saying, "The light of the body is the eye: if therefore thine eye be single, thy whole body shall be full of light" (Matthew 6:22). The eye represents our focus and our desires. When we have a singular focus on Christ, we can receive revelation and understanding, but when our eyes or heart resonates with other things, it brings darkness. Many believers have not grown in their relationship with Jesus as their Lord because they have failed to have the singular focus on him. Just as Paul severed his former devotions and affiliations, for us to walk in lordship, all of our former devotions must die. These devotions and affiliations are often reflected in our lifestyle choices—things such as devotion to political agendas, sorority or fraternity, religious organizations, gangs, devotion to a certain lifestyle, devotion to an individual, and the like. These and many other affiliations can drain the life of Christ out of a believer. Jesus will not be rivaled by any of our earthly affiliations or interests. The principle of lordship put in practice is simply, "I am for *what* Christ is for, and I am for *whom* Christ is for. I am against *what* Christ is against, and I am against *whom* Christ is against." My life is not an expression of my opinions and values; my life is a reflection of my Lord.

CHAPTER 3

Lordship Relationship: Loving the Lord

There is no person in the Bible who had a more prolific lordship relationship than David. From a young age, we find that David had a calling on his life to be Israel's King. David would be the divinely chosen leader of Israel. Of all the many people on the earth, God chose David to be his handpicked king. What was it about David that made him preferred by God? What made him a man after God's own heart? From an early age, we can easily see that it was his personal relationship to the Lord that set him apart. The prophet Samuel was sent to the home of David's father, Jesse, to anoint one of his sons to be king. Samuel went there excited about seeing the man who would make the leap from obscurity to notoriety and obtain the high office of being king of Israel. Samuel made the false assumption that this chosen individual would be easily recognizable. But the Lord was not pleased with Samuel's approach to his business. The issue the Lord had with Samuel was that Samuel gave consideration to the outer appearance or the physical stature of the man. That was not the way of the Lord. Samuel looked on Jesse's son Eliab and said, "Surely the Lord's anointed is before him" (1 Samuel 16:6). By his compulsive declaration, Samuel had technically pronounced Eliab as being God's chosen one. "But the Lord said unto Samuel, 'Look not on his countenance, nor on the height of his stature; because I have refused him: for the Lord seeth not as man seeth; for man looketh on the outward appearance, but the Lord looketh on the heart" (1 Samuel 16:7). This is an important lesson if we are going to have a relationship with the Lord. "The Lord looks on the heart." This means that the state of our hearts is vital to our relationship with the Lord. If we love the Lord from our hearts, relationship with him comes easy. If we are religious or self-serving, then distancing ourselves from the Lord will come naturally. David loved the Lord! It was this love for the Lord that made the Lord fall in love with David. To "love the Lord" is not just loving his goodness and his benefits. "Loving the Lord" is loving his authority, his Word, his precepts, his judgments, his commandments, and his statutes as well. In the last chapter, I wrote about how submission and obedience is essential to establishing a lordship relationship. In this chapter, you will see that loving the Lord is how one maintains that lordship relationship. Do you love the Lord?

Samuel anointed David that day "in the midst of his brethren," and "the Spirit of the Lord came upon David from that day forward" (1 Samuel 16:13). Notice that it is "the Spirit" of "the Lord." This is the divine Spirit that came from the throne room in heaven to assist David in accomplishing the will of the Lord. The Spirit of the Lord rests upon those who fear him and call him Lord. God rejected King Saul because Saul had not honored him as Lord in his choices and actions. Therefore, the scriptures report that "the Spirit of the Lord departed from Saul" (1 Samuel 16:14). This imposition of the presence of the Holy Spirit took David's relationship with the Lord to a whole new level. When David received the Holy Spirit, he began what has been referred to as his "training for reigning." David has already developed a love relationship with the Lord as a young lad. Although David had been anointed, he would spend many more years developing his relationship to the Lord before he would ever sit on a throne. Often the Lord shows you where you are going many years before you get there. He does this to keep you inspired. The way to promotion in the kingdom of God is to develop your relationship with the Lord. We can see the product of David's relationship with the Lord in his writing. In many of his psalms, David speaks of the Lord in the very first verse: "I will bless the LORD at all times, his praise shall continually be in my mouth" (Psalm 34:1). "The LORD is my shepherd, I shall not want" (Psalm 23:1). "The LORD is my light and my salvation, whom shall I fear?" (Psalm 27:1). These great verses of scripture are not simply the result of David having the presence of the Holy Spirit in his life. They are the outworking of the Holy Spirit in the life of a man who loves the Lord. There are many believers today who have the benefit of the Holy Spirit, but they do not love the Lord. In the end, we can simply say that David was chosen because he loved the Lord. This is lordship.

Goliath

One day, during his early years, as he was training for reigning, young David was sent to inquire about the welfare of his brothers who were out on the battlefield, fighting with the army of Israel. The Israelites were being intimidated by a giant named Goliath who was a part of the Philistine army. All of the Israelite men were afraid of Goliath because of his great size and stature. David said to them, "Let no man's heart fail him because of him [Goliath]; thy servant will go and fight with this Philistine" (1 Samuel 17:32). The men were amazed at David's confidence. They took him to King Saul. Saul said to David, "Thou art not able to go against this Philistine to fight with him: for thou art but a youth and he a man of war from his youth" (1 Samuel 17:33). David said to them, "The Lord that delivered me out of the paw of the lion, and out of the paw of the bear, he will deliver me out of the hand of this Philistine" (1 Samuel 17:37). This statement was evidence and testimony that David had grown in his relationship with the Lord. He had grown to trust that the Lord was present with him despite how adverse the circumstances were. Notice that David said, "The LORD who has delivered me out of the paw of the lion." David has had other incidents where he defeated a lion and a bear with the assistance of the Lord. This also means that David recognized what the Lord had done in his life. You will not grow in your lordship relationship until you determine to take note of what the Lord *has done* for you already, acknowledge what the Lord *is doing* in your life now, and trust him for what he *will do* in your future. As we spend time with the Lord, developing our relationship with him, we will learn to trust him for our deliverance, healing, salvation, and preservation. Because of David's confidence in the Lord, Saul sent him out to fight Goliath. When David went out on that battlefield to fight Goliath, he said to him, "You come to me with a sword and with a spear, and with a shield: but I come to you *in the name of the Lord* (emphasis mine)." David was not yet king of Israel, so this confession is not a reflection of him representing the people of God, but his language indicates a personal sense of lordship. We can easily see that it was David's sense of Jehovah as his Lord that made him fit to be the king of Israel! David further says, "This day, the Lord will deliver you into mine hand" (1 Samuel 17:45–46). It is obvious that David's confidence was not in himself; his confidence was in the Lord. All these things David had learned through an abiding lordship relationship.

> And David put his hand in his bag and took thence
> a stone and slang it and smote the Philistine in
> his forehead, that the stone sunk into his fore-
> head; and he fell to the earth. (1 Samuel 17:49)

That day, out on the battlefield, David took a sling and threw a certain stone at Goliath. This one stone was efficacious at killing Goliath. The stone literally sunk into Goliath's forehead. However, it was not David's strength that made the stone sink into the giant's head. This story is written so that we would see the assistance of the Lord in David's life. David casted the stone, but God turned the slingshot into a shotgun. The rock that was hurled at Goliath became a bullet by the grace and power of the Lord. This is the lordship relationship at work. The Lord assists those who honor him as their Lord. He does not force us to honor him as our Lord. It is a choice we must make ourselves. If we are satisfied with our religious practices, we will not develop a lordship relationship with Christ. But if we honor him as Lord over our lives, he will honor us with victories over our enemies.

The Lord's Anointed

Through military victory, David was promoted and became one of the servants of King Saul. This was God's way of advancing David and preparing him to be king. There are things you are going through right now that are nothing but preparation for God's unfolding plan in your life. King Saul promoted David, and out of envy, he simultaneously despised him. The lordship relationship is a mentoring relationship. God will allow you to have enemies present in your life to humble you and to teach you to rely on him. Saul's hatred for David was unwarranted. Saul was the king, and David was his servant. However, "Saul was afraid of David because the Lord was with him" (1 Samuel 18:12). The lordship relationship is perceptible. When you have an abiding relationship with the Lord, people will perceive it, just as Saul did with David. Other believers who love the Lord will honor you for it. However, the religious person will often be envious and persecute you for it. Even though Saul despised David, David viewed Saul through the lenses of his relationship with the Lord. When David was in the presence of Saul, "he conducted himself wisely in all his ways and the Lord was with him" (1 Samuel 18:14). This tells us that proper behavior before men is pleasing to the Lord. Promotion always comes from the Lord, but it often comes to us through men. Much persecution came to David because of Saul. Saul's envy toward David grew fierce. "And Saul sought to smite David even to the wall with a javelin; but he slipped away out of Saul's presence…and David fled and escaped that night. (1 Samuel 19:10) The malice and anger of Saul was at times overwhelming for David. Speaking to Saul's son Jonathan, David said, "As the Lord liveth, and as thy soul liveth, there is but a step between me and death" (1 Samuel 20:3). David knew that with just one misstep, he was as good as dead. It was at this point in David's life that we are allowed to see a very important aspect of David's relationship to the Lord. We are allowed to see that it was David's prayer life that sustained him through his trials.

Call unto me, and I will answer you, and show
you great and mighty things, which thou know-
est not. (Jeremiah 33:3)

Check with Me!

During this trying season of David's life when he was running
from Saul, we are allowed to get another glimpse into David's relationship to the Lord. It was during this season that David learned
to, "check with the Lord" on the decisions that he made. Under
great stress and pressure from Saul, David learned to pray prayers of
inquiry. This means that he learned to ask the Lord's opinion about
the decisions he made in his life. This is a very important part of the
lordship relationship. David and King Saul's relationship continued
to decline. David went from servant to Saul to being the enemy of
King Saul, running for his life. One day, David came to the city of
Nob; it was a city where the priest lived. David was in great distress
and fear. Fear gripped his soul, and consequently, he started operating in his flesh. In this state of mind, he was not able to properly
hear from the Lord. Therefore, David asked Ahimelech, the priest,
to inquire of the Lord for him. The believer who is under lordship
by faith turns to the Lord when he is under duress. The Christian
who does not know lordship will turn to himself, to man, or to the
world for relief. Saul's servant Doeg the Edomite was present that
day at Nob, and he informed King Saul of David's actions. "I saw the
son of Jesse coming to Nob, to Ahimelech the son of Ahitub. And
(Ahimelech) enquired of the Lord for him, and gave him victuals,
and gave him the sword of Goliath the Philistine" (1 Samuel 22:9–
10). Even in David's worst spiritual condition, he knew he needed
to hear from the Lord. How about you? Do you seek God's opinion
and input about your life?

A few years ago, God gave my wife a prophetic word. He said to
her, "You must check with me before you do a thing. Always check
with me! When you make decisions without checking with me, the
results you get take years off your life." David certainly understood
this principle. He knew that he needed to hear from God about his

life and his situation. Many saints have made a mess of their lives because God has had no input in the decisions that they have made. They erroneously believe in the god of their own intelligence. They took jobs without consulting God. They married people without consulting God. They made health-related decisions without consulting God. They make financial decisions without consulting God. Believers do these things because they do not have a proper lordship relationship to Christ.

Despite all of David's trials, the Lord showed himself faithful in David's life. While still running from Saul and living in the wilderness, David had amassed and trained a small group of fighting men. In 1 Samuel 23:1–2, David received word that the Philistines had come up to fight against the Israelites in Keilah and that they had robbed the threshing floor. David had fighting men with him. He also had the ability and skill to fight. However, these facts were not the primary reason he went into the battle. David enquired of the Lord, saying, "Shall I go and smite these Philistines?" And the Lord said, "Go!" This is called "consulting with the Lord." This is also called "checking with God." The believer who does not walk under lordship will make decisions based on their intellect. Modern believers in this same scenario would think, "I will go up to fight the Philistines because I've got more fighters than they have, and I can win," or they might say, "I will not go up and fight the Philistines because I think I will lose." This is how modern man operates: everything is done based on his intellect. There is no consulting the Lord. But God wants to teach his people to "check with him" on all decisions great and small because he wants to be Lord over our lives! When David was out of fellowship with the Lord, the priest consulted with God for him. This means that we must pray for others who are unsaved and for those believers who are weak. We must be priests to those who are out of fellowship with God. However, after David recovered himself, he no longer sought out a priest to consult the Lord for him, but he took up his own priesthood and sought the Lord himself. Revelation 1:6 says that Jesus Christ has "made us kings and priests unto God." There is no more need for you to seek out a priest. Learn to consult with the Lord for yourself. This is the lordship relationship.

Checking with the Lord is not simply seeking God for an affirmation of the things you already intend to do. Lordship implies submission to Christ. If Jesus is Lord, it means you will do what he tells you to do, even if it is contrary to your reasoning or wishes. Many times, I have desired to do a thing, but the Lord said, "No." If he is my Lord, then I will submit to his will. I can tell you that there were many times the Lord said, "No," and I was disappointed, only to be overjoyed later that I did not do it. When you check with the Lord, you will learn that the Lord knows best. There are many thoughts we get in our heads, and often we can feel very sure of what the outcome will be. But if Jesus is Lord, we will do what he says and not our own wishes. When was the last time you heard a believer say, "I wanted to do this thing…but the Lord said, 'No'"? When was the last time you heard a believer say, "I didn't want to do it, but I was led by the Lord to do it"? These occurrences should be common if we are having a lordship relationship with Christ. The real question becomes, "Is he Lord over your life or not?"

There are two things that you must walk in if you are going to practice checking with God. First, you must be humble. A proud man will not check with God because he prefers to believe that his intellect is just as good as the Lord's revelation. He is not humble enough to trust the Lord. This is what the scripture is referencing when it says, "Trust in the Lord with all your heart, and lean not to your own intellect" (Proverbs 3:5). The second thing you must master if you are going to check with God is that you must believe that God is for you and that his decisions are always for your betterment. Over the years, as I have submitted myself to the Lord, I have learned that not only are the Lord's decisions better than my own, but I have also learned to trust that he always has my best interests in mind. I can give you many examples of this in my life, but the examples in your own life will convince you more. David had learned to trust the Lord, and this is why he inquired of the Lord. He learned to trust God more than he trusted what he thought or what he saw in front of him. Under the new covenant, we have the Holy Spirit resident within us. Being led by the Holy Spirit requires the same respect for lordship as David displayed. The Holy Spirit is "the Spirit of the Lord." Therefore, all those who honor the Lord Jesus also honor his Spirit and are led by the Spirit. Apostle Paul, when telling of his missionary journeys, said, "After they were come to Mysia, they assayed to go into Bithynia: but the Spirit suffered them not" (Acts 16:7). This scripture shows us that the Holy Spirit was in on their deliberations. They were making decisions. They wanted to go to Bithynia, but the Spirit said, "No." This is the lordship relationship at work. We must be led of the Spirit, and we must still also check with the Lord in prayer. But someone may say, What if you pray but cannot discern or hear from the Lord? Not everyone has a prophetic ear. Some saints struggle with how to hear from God. Many Christian books have been written on the subject of how to hear from God. However, I will say this: when you cannot hear from God, you simply pray and wait. By wait, I mean you give God sacred time to give you a response or to guide you. You may not be the person who can quote what God has said to you verbatim, but you can certainly respectfully acknowledge God. Proverbs 3:6 says, "In all thy ways acknowledge him, and he will direct your path." Sometimes I have prayed and heard in my spirit a response from God. At other times, I had prayed and heard nothing, but God guided me into his will. The most important thing is that you acknowledge him as Lord over your life. Once you have prayed, offer God "sacred time" for him to lead you or to give you his direction. Sacred time will differ depending on the circumstances. Learn to acknowledge God and give him sacred time to lead you. If you start acknowledging the Lord, eventually you will start having impressions in your spirit concerning what he is speaking to you and concerning his will.

CHAPTER 4

The Will of God

God's will was expressed from the very beginning of recorded time. God created Adam and Eve and placed them in the garden of Eden. One of the most distinct characteristics of God's new created man was that he possesses a free will. This meant that Adam and Eve had the privilege of being able to choose to agree or dissent, even against God their Creator. Since God created man with free will, it was necessary that an expression of God's will be represented in the garden of Eden. The tree of the knowledge of good and evil was the first imposition of God's will upon man (Genesis 3:2–3). With this imposition of God's will, there came also a penalty. "Ye shall not eat of it, neither shall ye touch it, lest ye die" (Genesis 3:3) As long as Adam and Eve agreed with the commandment of God, they would not know the meaning of good and evil, and they would enjoy paradise. Thus, we can conclude that being in God's will is a type of living in paradise. However, Adam and Eve instead chose to exercise their free will and contradict God's commandment. The serpent tempted Eve first to question God's will. "Has God said ye shall not eat of the tree…?" (Genesis 3:1–5) When there was only God's will in the garden, there is no knowledge of good and evil. Once there were other "wills" in the garden, God's will becomes good and any other will is evil. Many people believe that the greatest struggle in the Christian life is personal sin. They often become overwhelmed with the fight against the flesh. We teach people that the goal is for them to stop sinning. But there is a bigger picture. The matter of individual sins is important, but it is only a small part of the picture. The bigger picture is the matter of doing God's will.

While the book of Genesis records man's rebellion against the righteous rule of God in the garden of Eden, the book of Isaiah records the rebellion of free will among the angels that were in heaven. Long before the existence of Adam and Eve, the angel Lucifer made a pronouncement. In a deliberate attempt to impose his own will, he declared:

> For thou hast said in thine heart, **I will** ascend into heaven, **I will** exalt my throne above the stars of God **I will** sit also upon the mount of the congregation, in the sides of the north: **I will** ascend above the heights of the clouds; **I will** be like the Most High. (Isaiah 14:13–14, emphasis added)

What is apparent in this scripture is that Lucifer had set his will against God. His reward for opposing God's will is also offered in the very next verse. "Yet thou shalt be brought down to hell, to the sides of the pit" (Isaiah 14:15). The principle of lordship is submission to God's will. The character of lordship is one who is determined to do God's will. The person who is under Christ's authority is not the Christian who uses the expression "the Lord." The believer who is walking under lordship is instead the one who does God's will. "Not everyone that saith unto me, Lord, Lord, shall enter into the kingdom of heaven; but he that doeth the Will of my Father which is in heaven" (Matthew 7:21). As a believer, you must begin to speak and confess that you will do God's will with your life. This is lordship. When you were born again, you received salvation from hell and eternal separation from God. But there is still your present life. What will you do with the days and years God has given you to live here on this earth? Many Christians have the mentality of "I will serve God when I get to heaven, but these years while I am living here on this earth, I will do my own will." If this is your mentality, you are standing on the same proverbial rock Lucifer stood on when he made his pronouncement in heaven. After the fall of Adam, man lost his will to obey God. The current state of mankind in his fallen Adamic nature is that he naturally sets his will against God. We do not naturally desire to do the will of God. Jesus came to earth to redeem us and to bring us back into a garden-of-Eden relationship with the Father. He came to redeem the will of man. Your body will go to the dust, but your soul and spirit have been redeemed. However, even as born-again and redeemed individuals, our flesh still rebels against the righteous rule of the Lord. Because of this, God has to assist us in learning to walk in the obedience that Adam and Eve had before the fall. "For it is God which worketh in you both to will and to do of his good pleasure" (Philippians 2:13). God is working in your life first to change your mentality and make you desire to do his will. Then even after you determine to do God's will, your flesh proves to be inadequate to carry out the will of God. Because of the weakness of the flesh, God has to also assist the believer who desires to do his will.

Jesus and God's Will

Every believer should know that Jesus came to this earth to die for our sins. But before Jesus died, he modeled for us the life of faith that he would expect from his followers. Therefore, if you want to know what God expects from your life as a believer, you must look at the life of Jesus. When we study the life of Jesus, we can see how determined Jesus was to do the will of his Father. Jesus came into this earth for one expressed reason, and that was to do God's will. Jesus bore witness to the Father's authority over himself and then set himself to do only those things that were pleasing to the Father. For the believer, the definition of lordship is the expression and witness of Christ's authority over your life. That expression and witness becomes invalid if the believer does his own will. The matter of God's will guided every action and decision of Jesus's earthly life. In John 5:30, Jesus says, "I can of mine own self do nothing: as I hear, I judge...because I seek not mine own will, but the will of the Father which hath sent me." Jesus's life was guided by the will of the Father and not by his own will. Thus, he modeled the purpose and vision for the believers' life. We are to live with an intentional determination to do God's will. This is lordship. In Matthew 12:46–50, Jesus was within a certain house teaching the people when his mother and brothers approached outside the building. The people informed Jesus of the arrival of his family, assuming he would stop what he was doing and receive them. "And one said unto him, 'Behold thy mother and thy brethren stand without, desiring to speak with thee" (Matthew 12:47). Their assumption was that Jesus's biological family would take priority over what he was currently doing. But Jesus corrected and redirected them on the matter, essentially saying that the "priority" for him was not biology but instead God's will. "For whosever shall do the will of my Father which is in heaven, the same is my brother, and sister, and mother" (Matthew 12:50). Jesus placed his devotion and priority on those believers who were sitting there in submission to him and hearing the word. It was these believers who were pleasing the Lord and who took precedence over even his own earthly family. We can see an even more explicit example of this at Gethsemane. Jesus knew that the time for him to go to the cross was drawing near. He did not desire it. Dying was contrary to his own will. He retreated to the Garden of Gethsemane to talk to the Father. Jesus prays, "Is there any other way, my Father?" (Matthew 26:39). His conclusion is right in step with lordship. "Nevertheless, not as I will but as thou wilt" (Matthew 26:39). All Jesus needed to know was that it was God's will, and the matter was settled. This is the type of devotion and submission the Father is seeking from you. This is lordship!

God's Word Is God's Will

Doing God's will is the most important thing you can do with your life. Some believers may say, "I don't know what God's will for my life is?" We should first know that the will of the Lord is not an instantaneous download of information but instead a progressive revelation. Romans 12:2 says, "And be not conformed to this world: but be ye transformed by the renewing of your mind, that ye may prove what is that good, and acceptable, and perfect will of God." There are two things about this scripture that the believer must grasp. The first is that the renewing of one's mind is directly related to him receiving more revelation of the will of God. If the believer has neglected the study of the Word of God, prayer, and the work of spiritual development, he will not know very much of what God's will is for his life. The will of God for the believer is progressive. As the believer is developed into Christian maturity, the will of God unfolds from good, to acceptable, to perfect. Apart from a prophetic revelation, no one can tell you the details of God's will for your life. Knowing God's will is a matter of staying connected to the Lord. Once the believer begins to engage the Word of God, he begins to have his first encounters with the will of God. Before he walks in the prophetic and revelatory will of God, he must first walk in the expressed will of God. God has expressed the rudimentary elements of his will in scripture. Therefore, when the believer begins to desire to know God's will for his life, he must start with the Word of God. There are some passages of scriptures in the Bible that specifically instruct us on what is God's will. 1 Thessalonians 5:18 says, "In everything give thanks, for this is the will of God in Christ Jesus concerning you." Here the believer is not told to "be thankful"; he is instead instructed to "give thanks" to God. This is God's will. No prophetic gift necessary. Consider 1 Thessalonians 4:3–5 that says, "For this is the will of God, even your sanctification that ye should abstain from fornication." The word *fornication* here means "sexual immorality." The will of God is clear here. It is God's will that the believer abstains from sexual immorality. We can see here that the first level of the believer's knowledge of the will of the God is simply engaging God's Word. There are many other scriptures in the Bible that express the manifested will of God although they may not explicitly use the phrase *the will of God*. For instance, when the Bible says, "Let us love one another" (1 John 4:7), these are not suggestions but the imposition of another aspect of God's will. It is God's will that we learn to love others. In this way, the Bible is our first step in perceiving and walking in the will of God.

While studying the Bible introduces the believer to God's will, as he walks in submission to the Lord, he will perceive more and more revelation of the specific will of the Lord for his life. God has many ways that he causes us to know his will. Here are a few of the ways the believer comes to know God's specific will for his life.

Prayer: Through simple prayer, the believer can perceive his Lord's will.

Inner witness: The believer can also know the will of God by the "inner witness" spoken of in 1 John 2:20, 27. The inner witness is nothing complicated. It simply means that the Holy Spirit inside the believer will "bear witness" of whether a thing is of God.

Led by the Holy Spirit: According to Romans 8:16, we can know we are doing God's will when we are being "led by the Holy Spirit."

Prophecy: The will of God can also be shown to us through prophecy. Prophecy may come through us or other believers.

Open/Closed doors: We may even know the will of God by open doors and closed doors. God often opens doors that are in his will and closes doors that are not. These are just some of the ways God gets his will to the individual believer.

Let us never doubt that we can know God's will, for the Bible explicitly says that we can. You can specifically know God's will for your life. Using these tools and others, you will become a reflection of the servant who knows his master's will. Colossians 1:9 says, "that ye might be filled with the knowledge of His will, in all wisdom and spiritual understanding." However, just the knowledge of God's will is not the goal. The final step is obedience. The word *obedience* means "to be determined to do as you are told." It is not the servant who knows God's will that pleases God but the servant who does God's will. In Luke 12:47, Jesus says, "And that servant which knew his Lord's will and prepared not himself, neither did according to his will shall be beaten with many stripes." If you fail to acknowledge the lordship of Jesus over your life, you will not know God's specific will. You may boast of your Bible knowledge, but you will still lack divine vision for your personal life. Servants who live under the lordship of Christ know what the specific will of the Lord is for their lives. Not being in God's will has caused many saints to die with the

Bible right in their hands. They did not submit to Jesus as LORD, and consequently, they died living off human reasoning. Only through submission and obedience can we manifest the kingdom of God in our lives. This is lordship!

God facilitates what is in his will.

Gideon

In the book of Judges chapter 6, we find a certain Israelite man named Gideon. Gideon was a man caught in a dilemma. His country had been invaded by tribal hordes of Midianites. The Israelite people were hiding in caves from these Midianites to preserve their lives (Judges 6:1–2) Gideon was just a young man at this time. He too was in hiding from these Midianites. He was hastily threshing wheat by the winepress to hide it from the Midianites, when he had a visit from an angel of God (Judges 6:11). The angel appeared to him suddenly with a word from God. "The Lord is with thee, thou mighty man of valor," said the angel. This was a very positive confession in a very negative circumstance. Gideon's response was typically appropriate. "If the Lord be with us, then why has all this befallen us?" (Judges 6:13) That was a great question! It is often those paradoxical moments in life that force us to seek out and understand God's will. Those moments in life when we are under the attack of the enemy. Those moments when we have no answers for what is assailing us. This angel told Gideon that he would single-handedly save Israel from the hording Midianites (Judges 6:14). This idea sounded wonderful to Gideon but simultaneously problematic. Gideon heard from the angel, but he needed a greater confirmation from God before he was willing to go to war against the Midianites. Gideon was a believer, and there was a part of him that knew that God could deliver Israel. However, Gideon needed to be absolutely sure that what the angel said to him was God's will. What Gideon did next has become a very common proverb when speaking of knowing God's will. In Judges 6:36–40, Gideon entreated the Lord concerning the angel's testimony. Gideon was not a spirit-filled man; therefore, there was no "inner witness" or "prophecy" to look to. Gideon would need something much more practical. He employed a fleece of wool, and he prayed to God, "If thou will save Israel by my hand, as thou has said, Behold I will put this fleece of wool on the ground and if the dew be upon the fleece only, and the earth be dry. Then shall I know that thou will save Israel" (Judges 6:37). You cannot blame Gideon for wanting this assurance. He wanted to do as the angel had instructed, but he also needed to be assured he was in the will of God. God obliged the young man. The next morning, the fleece was full of water, and the surrounding ground was completely dry. God gave Gideon his confirmation. But Gideon was not quite finished. Maybe his scientific mind could reason how the dew could fall in a certain place and give him a false positive. Gideon needed a second test to ensure he was truly discerning God's will. Therefore, Gideon entreated the Lord once again. He said, "Lord don't be angry, but let's do the test another way. This time, I will put the fleece out again, but I want you to allow the fleece to remain dry but the ground around it to be wet with dew (Judges 6:39). The next morning, the situation was according to Gideon's request. The fleece was dry, but the ground all around the fleece was wet with dew. Gideon did all these things, seeking to discern the will of the Lord. Many believers have viewed Gideon's actions as faithless. However, when the answer to your question will send you hopelessly into a war you cannot win without the assistance of God, you would want to be sure also!

But you don't have to be facing war to desire to know God's will. You need to know God's will on what college you should attend. You need to know God's will on who you should marry. You need to know God's will on where you should live. There are many daily activities that God's people need to do a much better job of entreating God to know his will. Personal pride is a hindrance to the will of God. When a person is walking in pride, he does not desire to know God's will. This is the state of many believers today. They are impressed with their own intellect and reasoning, and they desire to live their lives without the opinion of God. Thus, they shun the matter of seeking to know God's will. Gideon did not have the spiritual discernment to know God's will on the matter, so he did what he had to do to connect with God and get some answers. This was commendable. However, there are many believers today who do not have discernment to know God's will on a matter, and they instead resort to sources such as mediums, psalm readers, witchcraft, and the kingdom of darkness for direction. Thus, their latter end is worse than the former. When they simply did not know God's will, the Lord could have assisted them. But when they turned to the kingdom of darkness for answers, they have betrayed the Lord and his wisdom for the wisdom of devils.

God's will is God's bill.

Peter's Boat

And Simon answering said unto him, Master, we have
toiled all the night, and have taken nothing: nevertheless,
at thy word, I will let down the net. (Luke 5:5)

In Luke chapter 5, Jesus entreated Peter for the use of his boat. At the time Jesus addressed Peter, he had already been fishing for many hours. Jesus approached Peter in the morning hours while Peter and his men were busy washing their fishing nets. This matter of washing fishing nets was done by fishermen at the end of a shift before they left the lake for home. Peter obliged Jesus and consented to allow him to use the boat. Jesus used Peter's boat as a stage to preach the word of God to the anxious crowd standing on the lakeside. After the preaching of the word, Jesus instructed Peter to "launch out into the deep water again and recast the nets" (Luke 5:4). Peter did not desire to go back out into deep water, nor did he want to recast his nets after they had just been cleaned. But those who are under lordship do what the Lord says, even when the Lord's commands are contrary to their own will. Peter did express to Jesus, "We have toiled all the night and have taken nothing" (Luke 5:5). But something inside of Peter sensed that the command to return to deep waters came from a Greater Authority than himself. Peter's confession of useless toiling turns into, "Nevertheless, at thy word, I will let down the net" (Luke

5:5). One of the evidences of a person being out of God's will is toil. Is your life a constant toil? Believers who are not in God's will, will toil even in waters that others are flourishing in. This is not to say that being in God's will is always easy. It is not. However, "toil" is the production of the flesh. Toil is the believer trying to do it himself instead of relying on the Lord. Toiling to pay bills. Toiling in relationships. Toiling in work. There is a physical toil, and there is a psychological toil. Peter had been fishing in his own strength. But now he was going to return to the deep waters "at thy word" and, consequently, in God's will. The command to return to deep waters and recast the fishing nets was also contrary to Peter's experience and intelligence. As Peter submitted to the lordship of Jesus, he came into the Lord's will and also began to receive his inheritance. "And when they had done this, they enclosed a great multitude of fishes: and their net brake" (Luke 5:6). This is lordship! The Christian life done by intelligence is toil. If you have not learned to do life "at his will," yours will be a life of toil, no matter how intelligent you may be. Many Christians today are angry with the Lord because they have taken so many hits from the devil. They have toiled so much that they are weary. Many of God's children need to stop trying to be an intelligent Christian and learn to be a believer! Many need to determine to find and walk in God's will for their life. This is lordship.

The safest place in the whole wide world is in the will of God.

Abraham

> Now the Lord had said unto Abram, Get thee out of thy country, and from thy kindred, and from thy father's house, unto a land that I will shew thee: And I will make of thee a great nation, and will bless thee, and make thy name great; and thou shalt be a blessing. And I will bless them that bless thee, and curse them him that curse thee: and in thee shall all the families of the earth be blessed. So Abram departed as the Lord had spoken to him.

In Genesis 12:1–4, God imposed his will on a man named Abram. God said to Abram, "Get away from your country and your kindred." With this command, God brings Abram from simply being a believer to walking under lordship. Even in the Old Testament, the men and women whom God used were required to have a lordship relationship to God. As I have already stated in previous chapters, the lordship relationship demands submission and obedience. Abram responded to the Lord commandment with blind obedience. "So Abram departed as the Lord had spoken." This is lordship. There is much we can learn from Abraham's lordship relationship. Firstly, we can see that lordship is doing God's will even when you do not know the outcome. Too many Christians want God to give them a road map and an itinerary of activities so that they can see if they agree with the agenda. If Abram had called God his Lord but did not leave his father's house, would that be lordship? We can also see that God's will for Abram was not relegated to spiritual things. God did not ask him to pray or worship or preach. God commanded that he pack his things and move out. God's will for Abram and for you and I is intimately weaved into your personal and practical lives. Abram was willing to make sacrifices and to expend energy and effort into getting into God's will—and so must you. Just as it was with Jesus in the Garden of Gethsemane, we must realize that God's will can often be objectionable to our flesh. God told Abram to get away from the people he loved. I would not doubt that he did this with some emotional strain. Abram left his country and his kinfolk behind, in search of God's will for his life. He did not know the full plan of God when he went out, but he went out trusting the Lord. Much effort must be put into getting into God's will. Finally, we must know that the reward of the Lord is with him. When a person resolves to do God's will, God also resolves to bless them. Hebrews 11:6 tells us that "he is a rewarder of them who diligently seek him." Abram left Ur, seeking to do God's will. However, he also left with this promise, "And I will make of thee a great nation, and I will bless thee, and make thy name great; and thou shalt be a blessing" (Genesis 12:2). Lordship is not all sacrifice and suffering. Just as we have seen with Peter and his boat, after obedience, there is success! He left that place as a man named Abram, but through submission and obedience, he became Father Abraham.

> Prophetic Word: "I cannot bless you when you are not in my will because if I bless you and you are not in my will, you will assume that you are doing the right things."

God has to refrain from blessing the Christian who is not in his will. If God prospers you and you are in a false religion, you will assume that, that religion is correct. You will say, "I am right with my faith because I see the manifestation of God's blessings on my life." If God blesses you and you are in sexual immorality, you will assume that sexual immorality is acceptable with God. Therefore, God must withhold blessings from you until you seek out and get fully into his will. This is the frustration of many Christians. They know there is more. They desire more from God. But they are not under lordship, and they do not seek God's will for their lives. The blessings of the Lord become a sign to you that God is in agreement with the life you are living. Conversely, if you are not blessed, there is some area of your life where you are not fully in his will. I have known of people who were not yet saved who were seeking blessings from God. If you are not saved through the blood of the Lord Jesus Christ, you are certainly not in God's will. I was teaching on the will of God and how God withholds blessings from believers when one of my students said, "Why should you do right when you are being rewarded for doing wrong?" I could not have said it any better. Many believers are angry with God because they realize he has not manifested for them as they wished he would. God must withdraw his grace from you because he does not want to persuade you to continue down the road you are on. Therefore, one of the signs that you are not in God's will is that you cannot find grace, favor, or blessings. In addition to this, there is often a timing to when God chooses to bless you. God often releases blessings to you as "evidence" that you are on his road and in his will. For instance, it is God's will that a certain Christian man work on his marriage. That man finally agrees with

God and starts making the effort to win his wife back. Suddenly and inexplicably, he is offered a free vacation for two to a coveted island destination. Coincidence? No, this is God's way of "evidencing" to him that he is doing God's will. God will also bless you in a timing to testify that there is something you are doing that he is pleased with. Conversely, God withholding grace or blessings should make you question whether your life is pleasing to God. When I cannot pay my bills, I am either under attack from the enemy, or I am out of God's will. This principle was often expressed in the Old Testament by God withholding rain. Rain is a type of God's blessings. When there was drought or famine, it was often God's way of protesting the actions of his people.

> If I shut up heaven and there be no rain, or if I command the locust to devour the land, or if I send pestilence among my people. If my people who are called by my name shall humble themselves and pray, and seek my face, and turn from their wicked ways; then will I hear from heaven, and will forgive their sin and will heal their land. (2 Chronicles 7:13–14)

God's blessings for your life are already in his will. When you are in his will, there are many things you will not even have to pray for. This is lordship!

CHAPTER 5

War with the World

In its simplest sense, lordship is accountability to Christ. Lordship is living the Christian life with the same sense of accountability to the Lord Jesus as he modeled for us to the Father. Worldliness is the enemy of Christian accountability. But what is worldliness? Worldliness is the subversion of the believer's witness before men by his conformity to the world. Ephesians 2:2 says, "Wherein in time past ye walked according to the course of this world, according to the prince of the power of the air, the spirit that now works in the children of disobedience." In this scripture, Satan is called the prince or ruler of this world. He holds this title because he possesses an influential authority over the people of this world. The word "world" does not reference the earth we are standing upon. The world can be defined as a system of ideals and behaviors that have derived from man in his sinful state under the leadership of Satan. To put it another way, *worldly* is the description of the believer who lacks accountability to his Lord but instead maintains conformity to the natural ways of men. Worldliness is pervasive among Christians in American society. Christ calls the believer to renounce the world. In John 16:33, Jesus announced that he had overcome the world, and so it must be with the believer. He must subdue the spirit of the world and place himself under Christ's authority. I have given you a definition of worldliness, but there are other questions about the matter of worldliness that always seem to follow. How do you know worldliness when you see it? What exactly is the problem with the world? Why is the world such a bad thing? Is worldliness anything we are doing that the unsaved person does also? Is worldliness taking a trip to Walmart? Is it worldly to go to a theme park or to the beach? Furthermore, how does the believer eschew the world? Let us take a short journey into this matter of worldliness so that we can get some answers to these and other questions.

There is "sinful," and then there is "worldly." Both are explicitly spoken against in scripture, but they are not necessarily the same. Sinfulness has to do either with things we have been forbidden to do or the things that we are commanded to do that we leave undone. Worldliness, on the other hand, is a state of mind in the believer. A Christian is not worldly because he attends an office party or goes to a theme park. Although if he goes to an office party and gets drunk on alcohol, this would be considered sinful. Worldliness has to do with the believer's disposition about the things of this world. When the believer loves the ways of this world or the things of this world, his heart turns to compliance with the world, and he forsakes the standards of the Lord. Worldliness is living a life of self-pleasure. Worldliness is the believers' failure to die to this world and live their lives to the glory of God.

> Love not the world, neither the things that are
> in the world. If any man love the world, the love
> of the Father is not in him. For all that is in the
> world, the lust of the flesh, and the lust of the
> eyes, and the pride of life, is not of the Father, but
> is of the world. (1 John 2:15–16)

> If ye then be risen with Christ, seek those things
> which are above, where Christ sitteth on the right
> hand of God. Set your affection on things above,
> not on things on the earth. For ye are dead, and
> your life is hid with Christ in God. (Colossians
> 3:1–3)

Some Christians have fallen in love with this world as is indicated in the first scripture above. Other believers have maintained a sense of lordship and are seeking the things that are above. The world we live in is evil. Galatians 1:4 says that Jesus "gave himself for our sins, that he might deliver us from this present evil world, according to the will of God and our Father." Although the world we live in is evil, it does not prevent it from being appealing. Thus, the believer must "die to this world." The believer must be deliberate in his intention to live for Christ. If the believer's life begins to conform to the things of this world, he has become useless to the Lord Jesus. In 2 Timothy 4:10, Paul writes, "Demas has forsaken me, having loved this present world and has departed unto Thessalonica." Here we see what happens when the believer falls in love with the world. He abandons the things of God and separates himself from the ministry. If the world that Paul lived in was appealing enough to cause Demas to defect, then we must know that today's world is even more appealing. This modern world with its money, cell phones, fancy cars, restaurants, nightlife, expensive homes, five-star hotels, television shows, fine clothing, airplanes, and parties has caused many believers to lose their light. Demas is not the only believer who has "departed" from the calling of God to pursue the world. None of the things I have just listed are inherently sinful in and of themselves. God blesses people with fancy homes, money, cars, and so forth. Worldliness is a spirit. It is a love of the current world in your heart that rises up and makes the believer forsake his walk with the Lord and the future hope that is in Christ Jesus.

God versus Mammon

No man can serve two masters: for either he will
hate the one, and love the other; or else he will
hold to the one, and despise the other. Ye cannot
serve God and mammon. (Matthew 6:24)

Nothing draws a Christian into worldliness faster than the love of money. This one word, *money*, has been the downfall of many believers. Your disposition toward money can also reflect whether there is worldliness in your heart. In the scripture above, *mammon* is best interpreted as "wealth." "Ye cannot serve God and wealth." However, it can also be interpreted as "greed." Having money is not inherently sinful. There are many believers who have wealth and who walk under lordship. However, if the Christian's desire for money is driven by a lust for the things of this world, he is in the service of mammon. He has become worldly. Let us make no mistake here; this is the condition of many believers today. Whether he is a Christian who is spending his money at the gambling casinos and sports betting, or the Christian who sits all day watching the stock market because he has no faith in God to provide for him, they are both in service to the spirit of mammon. The scripture above says that when this condition exists in a person, he will "hate the one, and love the other, or he will hold to the one and despise the other." When a Christian is worldly, he will secretly hate God and love the world. Many Christians resist the Lord Jesus reigning over their lives because in their hearts is a drive for a kingdom of their own. They are not servants of God; they are servants of money!

Compliance and Conformity

> And be not conformed to this world: but be ye
> transformed by the renewing of your mind, that
> ye may prove what is that good, and acceptable,
> and perfect, will of God. (Romans 12:2)

The spirit of the world is compliance and conformity. The scripture above says, "be not conformed to this world." There is an invisible force operating in this world. It is an implicit call to conform and to embrace the character of those who are of the world. This "force" to conform must be resisted by the believer. Paul, when speaking of the spirit of the world, said this, "But God forbid that I should glory, save in the Cross of our Lord Jesus Christ, by whom the world is crucified unto me, and I to the world" (Galatians 6:14). The believer is crucified with Christ. He is to die to this sinful world. If the believer is still alive to the world and its ways, he has become worldly. Christ saves the believer out of the world and calls the believer to himself. This means that the life the believer lives must glorify God. 2 Corinthians 5:15 says, "He died for all, so that they which live should no longer live unto themselves, but unto him which died for them and rose again." The world with its system of ideals and behaviors are contrary to lordship.

> If the world hate you, ye know that it hated me before it hated you. If ye were of the world, the world would love his own: but because ye are not of the world, but I have chosen you out of the world, therefore the world hates you. (John 15:18–19)

The world hates the Lord Jesus, but that does not mean that the world hates religion. Religion is quite acceptable to those who are of the world. Let us be clear. Jesus specifically said that the world "hates me." The believer must not fail to see this point. All of the religions of the world are at war with one person—Christ. When the believer comes into contact with people who are conformed to this world, he will find a natural resistance, resentment, and hatred for the Lord Jesus. Consequently, he will find a natural resistance, resentment, and hatred for his compliance to the Lord Jesus. The more under lordship the believer is, the deeper the resentment he will find. Jesus has already informed us of the attitude the world will always have toward the believer. This is where the matter of conformity to the world begins. The believer has to make a decision as to whether his conversations, actions, and manner of life will reflect lordship or conformity to the world. If he chooses conformity, he will receive some level of acceptance from the people of the world. If his chooses lordship, he will be resented by the men of the world but accepted by those believers who embrace lordship. Jesus never told us to seek to be accepted by the people of this world. Many modern-day television shows express blasphemy toward the Lord Jesus and resistance to the ways of God. As a believer, you will often find that it is not the heathen person who will persecute you for your belief in Christ. More often it is the religious person who will resent your standard of behavior and lordship. The spirit of worldliness is the desire to be accepted by man. The modern church has even yielded to the spirit of the world. Driven by a lust for success and not understanding worldliness, many modern-day pastors seek to make the things of God appealing to the people of the world. The work of the church should be that of calling men out of the world. The only way we can effectively call men out of the world is to have no hint of the world in our churches. Instead, we have chosen to make the church consistent with the world. When the goal of the church has become being popular to the people of the world, we lose our light. The purpose of "light" is to allow men to see when they are in darkness. The purpose of "light" is to be different from the darkness. Turning on the light dispels the darkness. But when there is no difference between those of the light and those in darkness, how can anyone be saved?

The Image of the World

"Then the princes, the governors, and captains, the judges, the treasures, the counselors, the sheriffs, and all the rulers of the provinces, were gathered together unto the dedication of the image that Nebuchadnezzar the king had set up; and they stood before the image that Nebuchadnezzar had set up. And a herald cried aloud, To you it is commanded, O people, nations, and languages, That at what time ye hear the sound of the cornet, flute, harp, sackbut, psaltery, dulcimer, and all kinds of music, ye fall down and worship the golden image that Nebuchadnezzar the king hath set up: And whoso falleth not down and worship shall the same hour be cast into the midst of a burning fiery furnace." (Daniel 3:3–6)

As I stated earlier, the spirit of the world is compliance and conformity. There are many examples of this in scripture. In Daniel chapter 3, there is the story of three Hebrew men named Shadrach, Meshach, and Abednego. This story is a textbook example of how persecution from the world comes to the believer when he is under lordship. In the story, King Nebuchadnezzar made a statue of gold and demanded that all the people in his providence worship the image. When the believer engages the world, his values are put at risk. The believer has to make many decisions about life that are a matter of the intersection between the world and his accountability to his Lord. Consequently, the believer must have a biblical perspective on both social and political issues. After King Nebuchadnezzar made his edict, the people of the province did conform to and comply with the king's mandate. "All the people, the nations, and the languages, fell down and worshipped the golden image that Nebuchadnezzar the king had set up" (Daniel 3:7). Everyone was in compliance to Nebuchadnezzar's idol. This is the spirit of the world. We should always be aware that pressure to conform that comes from the world has many forms. Many people of status, wealth, and popularity are following Satan through the spirit of the world. If the believer seeks to be popular or have standing with the people of this world, he will yield to this influence and renounce his devotion to Christ. Many believers have placed their faith in the closet, seeking to find status and acceptance among the men and women of this world.

Music

After Nebuchadnezzar set up the image, he made an announcement that all the people should worship the image. In addition to his commandment, he added the imposition of music. Not just a little music, he wanted "all kinds of music." Music is appealing to people. God created us with the unique ability to create and to appreciate music. However, the enemy seeks to use music to inculcate his demonic values into the world. Music is a tool of the enemy. There is much "devil music" in this world. The enemy uses rock, R&B, reggae, rap, heavy metal, even Christian music that has been produced by men who are not under lordship—literally "all kinds of music." I was counseling with a young man who was in prison for murder. He had given his life to Jesus while in prison. I asked him quite frankly, "Why did you kill that man?" He said, "I was listening to that gangster rap music, and through it, the enemy had filled me with demons." Music is influential. In the Daniel chapter 3 story, the music did not just represent something for the people to listen to while they worship the image. The music represented the very influence of the world through the evil one. This is why in the church, the person who sits at the piano or keyboard must be under lordship. It is better to have a novice who is under lordship than an extremely talented person who is servant to the idols of the world.

In the Daniel chapter 3 story, all of the people were worshipping the image except these three Hebrew men, Shadrach, Meshach, and Abednego. Perhaps those who were worshipping the image could have said, "Don't worry about those three Hebrew guys. They don't matter." Instead, the scripture gives us another account. "Wherefore at that time, certain Chaldeans came near [to Nebuchadnezzar] and accused the Jews" (Daniel 3:8). These Chaldeans told the king that Shadrach, Meshach, and Abednego were not in compliance and were not conforming to his demand. This is the spirit of persecution that comes from people of the world. Because of their testimony to King Nebuchadnezzar, these Hebrew men had to be thrown into a fiery furnace. If you read your Bible, I do not have to give you a line-by-line account of the rest of the story. You can read it yourself. However, we should know that their confession to Nebuchadnezzar before they were thrown into the furnace was, "Our God whom we serve is able to deliver us from the burning fiery furnace… But even if he does not…we will not serve your gods, nor worship the golden image that you have set up!" This is lordship! God used this story to show us both the persecution that comes from the world and his faithfulness to those who stand under lordship. The world does not like the presence of those who represent the Lord Jesus and his kingdom. They know that Christ's kingdom is against the world and that the world is against Christ's kingdom.

Jericho

And ye, in any wise keep yourselves from the accursed thing, lest ye make yourselves accursed, when ye take of the accursed thing, and make the camp of Israel a curse, and trouble it. (Joshua 6:18)

And Achan answered Joshua, and said, Indeed I have sinned against the Lord God of Israel, and thus and thus have I done: When I saw among the spoils a goodly Babylonish garment and two hundred shekels of silver, and a wedge of gold of fifty shekels weight, then I coveted them, and took them: and behold they are hid in the earth in the midst of my tent, and the silver under it. (Joshua 7:20–21)

Jericho was the first city the Israelites came to when they entered into the promised land. This city of Jericho was to be totally dedicated to the Lord. Nothing inside the city was to be taken; the entire city was devoted to God. We often use this story to teach the principle of the tithe and firstfruits. However, the Jericho story has quite a vivid picture of worldliness. Before the conquest of Jericho, the Israelites were sternly warned not to touch anything in the city. An Israelite man named Achan violated this rule when he entered the city. He kept some things that he found within the city for himself. In doing this, Achan became a type of the worldly Christian. He was with God's people, but he loved the things of this world. The premise of his worldliness was his love for things. Achan took from the city three things: (1) Babylonian garment, (2) silver, and (3) gold. What is also interesting is that after his deed was exposed, in Achan's confession he plainly said, "I coveted them." There are many worldly Christians who covet material things. But Achan did not just covet money; he also coveted the Babylonian garment. There is a spiritual interpretation to the term *garments*. Garments represent how other people view you. Garments represent "social significance." Garments are a type of "glory among men" or "desire for fame." Furthermore, it was not a Hebrew garment he desired, but a "Babylonian" garment that Achan coveted. If you study the etymology of Babylon, you will find that Babylon always represents "the world." Thus, Achan represents the worldly believer. This spirit is still among us today. There are believers all around us who have a lust for material things or for fame. They want to be internet stars, television stars, church stars, porn stars, and so forth. They want to be recognized by the men and women of this world. They covet the garments of this world. When the believer has embraced the world, he cannot possess the love of the Father. 1 John 2:15 says, "Love not the world… If any man love the world, the love of the Father is not in him." This scripture has two directives. If a man loves the world, he cannot love God the way he should. He cannot serve two masters. However, this same scripture also implies that when a man loves the world, he cannot be a reservoir of God's love. He cannot properly love people. Instead of being a display of God's love in the world, he instead becomes a friend of the world.

Walk in the Light

Satan is "the god of this world" (2 Corinthians 4:4). His work is that of keeping people lost and estranged from God. The enemy employs many ways and means of keeping the unsaved "blinded." God saves the believer and calls the saint to be a light in the midst of this dark world. Contrarily, the enemy desires to maintain the darkness so that men would die in their sins. Once you have been born again, you are a candle that has been lit for Christ Jesus. You have the potential to influence others, but only if you are under the light of lordship. After salvation, you are positioned to be a light to the world. (Matthew 5:14–16). The born-again believer provides the light for those who walk in darkness. Satan is enemy to the believer who is "shining." The war with the world is a battle for the light. Philippians 2:15 says, "That ye may be blameless and harmless, the sons of God without rebuke, in the midst of a crooked and perverse nation, among whom ye shine as lights in the world." However, if the believer embraces the standards, values, and morals of the world, he blends in, and the effect is like a barrel that is placed over a candlestick. "Neither do men light a candle, and put it under a bushel, but on a candlestick: and it giveth light unto all that are in the house" (Matthew 5:15). The believer ceases to give light when he is worldly. The work of the enemy is to make the world appealing to the believer, to make the believer renounce his devotion to Christ, and consequently, suppress his light.

The Believer's Heart

Every believer is to be mentored by the Lord. The Christian who rejects lordship grows callous to the presence of the Lord. The believer who is accepting of lordship remains sensitive to the Lord's conviction. Because he is under lordship, he can be convicted or corrected by the Lord at any time. The Holy Spirit will convict him of sin that is in his life. The Lord will also convict him when he is inappropriate, proud, or worldly. The believer who is under lordship will find himself saying to someone, "I want to apologize for my behavior yesterday" or "The Lord really convicted me of the things I said to my husband" or "I had to ask forgiveness." These moments will be common for any believer who is walking under the lordship of Christ. I was talking with a certain young Christian woman when she unexpectedly said, "God keeps testing me!" I said, "Do you mean he is testing your faith?" She replied, "No, God keeps testing me to see if I am with him or with the world." This young believer was being dealt with by Christ. Christ demands those who are his to live faithful lives. This young lady knew intuitively that it was the world that the Lord was chastising her about. Her faith in Christ was being tested. Christ was calling her to overcome the world. "Everyone who has been born of God overcomes the world. And this is the victory that overcomes the world even our faith" (1 John 5:4). The born-again believer must know that his Lord is alive and well. His faith has to stand up in a world that seeks to seduce the believer.

I began the chapter talking about how we know worldliness when we see it. Worldliness is not any particular act but instead has to do with the disposition of the believer's heart as he engages the world. Therefore, worldliness is not going to a party or watching a movie. Worldliness is not attending a show or going on vacation. Worldliness has to do with the value the believer places on Christ being Lord over his life and the witness of that reality to others. There are many things that can be participated in without a violation of lordship. Worldliness has to do with the state of the believer's heart, and not necessary the description of the acts. Paul implied this when he said, "All things are lawful to me, but not all things are beneficial" (1 Corinthians 10:23). In its simplest sense, worldliness is a Christian who has lost his witness. He has not maintained a conscious witness of Christ as Lord of his life in his choices, actions, and decisions.

THE ONENESS OF CHRIST

━━━━━━━━━━━━━━━━━━━━━

CHAPTER 6

━━━━━━━━━━━━━━━━━━━━━

Stewardship

The earth is the Lord's and the fullness thereof.
The world, and they that dwell therein.

—Psalm 24:1

For many people, Psalm 24:1 is merely poetry. However, for those of us who have a revelation of lordship, this verse has significant meaning. Everything on this earth belongs to the Lord! It is hard for some people to take this verse literally because Jesus is not always walking around pointing at things, saying, "This is mine" and "That is mine." If we truly owned anything, we would be able to take it with us when we died. But if you died today, you would leave everything behind. The sad thing is that the person who receives it after you die will probably also believe that he owns it too. At its root, stewardship simply means "I own nothing." We never own anything during our brief stay here on this earth. God loans to us what is his so that we can live our lives and complete our earthly assignment. Everything we receive in this life, whether we work for it or it is gifted to us, belongs to the Lord. This is the first principle of stewardship. Stewardship is a natural consequence of lordship. If Jesus is my Lord, then I am his steward. If Jesus is not my Lord, then I am not a steward. A proud man cannot receive this truth. Psalm 24:1 says that "the earth is the Lord's." There are many people who will concede that the ground they are standing on belongs to God. But the verse also says, "and the fullness thereof." This means everything within the earth belongs to the Lord. Then it goes further to say, "the world, and the people who dwell in it." This leaves nothing for us to own. Everything belongs to the Lord Jesus. Colossians 1:16 says, "For by him were all things created, that are in heaven, and that are in earth, visible and invisible, whether they be thrones, or dominions or principalities or powers: all things were created by him and for him." This verse cannot simply be consented to. God's children must receive this truth by revelation. The idea that Jesus is Lord must be believed and expanded upon. If Jesus is Lord, then he owns all things, even our lives. 1 Corinthians 6:19 says, "Know ye not that your body is the temple of the Holy Ghost, which is in you, which ye have of God, and ye are not your own?" We don't even own the bodies we reside in. We are only stewards of things that ultimately belong to God.

As believers, we are stewards of God's resources. This revelation proceeds prosperity. The best analogy for stewardship I can give you is that of a grocery store manager. The store manager does not own the products in the store. However, he has control and governing authority over those things for the purpose of promoting the owner's interests. When I first received this teaching on stewardship, my flesh rebelled against it. I did not like the idea of thinking that my car belongs to God, my house belongs to God, my wife belongs to God. In my mind, these were things I had worked for and earned. God led me to make confessions out of my mouth, out loud, where my ears could hear it. I began to confess, "This house I live in belongs to the Lord!" "This money I have belongs to God." "This car I drive belongs to the Lord." "This company I work for belongs to God." "I belong to God." As I kept confessing it out of my mouth, my soul and my spirit came into agreement with that truth. The first principle of stewardship is that you must acknowledge that what you have received in this life is from the Lord. It belongs to the Lord, and it will be returned to the Lord. Whether it is two pennies or ten million dollars, God has made you steward over his resources. The second principle of stewardship is that you must value what you have been given. Everything you have is an endowment from the Lord. Your talents, gifts, and abilities are all endowments. Even your intelligence has been granted. Your appreciation for what God has given you will determine how much more God assigns to you. If you see your car as an endowment from God, then the maintenance and upkeep of that car becomes a part of your stewardship. If you view your spouse as a gift from God, then how you treat them becomes a part of your stewardship. This list goes on and on.

A Revelation of Stewardship

To help us get a better revelation of stewardship, let us look once again at God's servant David. Before David was anointed to be king, he was a young lad out in the fields, attending to the sheep. It was there that God would teach him stewardship of the animals before he would become the steward of the nation of Israel. We can see one of David's stewardship lessons when he was sent by his father, Jesse, to take his brothers victuals. The Bible says, "And David rose up early in the morning and left the sheep with a keeper" (1 Samuel 17:20). This shows us that David had learned to be responsible for the things God had place in his care. The sheep must be cared for even if he has to go away. Shepherding the sheep was David's employment at that time. All employment is stewardship. You have been contracted as a steward by your employer to do a certain task. How you perform that work is a reflection of your stewardship to God. The scripture says, "Servants be obedient to them that are your masters [bosses] according to the flesh, with fear and trembling, in singleness of heart, as unto Christ" (Ephesians 6:5). Pastoring a church is the stewardship of God's people. And it is one of the highest stewardship callings anyone can receive. "Take heed therefore unto yourselves, and to all the flock, over the which the Holy Ghost hath made you overseers, to feed the church of God which he has purchased with his own blood" (Acts 20:28). If you have the care of even an animal, it is a part of your stewardship. God wants you to treat that animal well. There are many people who believe that God is only concerned with our salvation, spiritual things, and heaven. They believe he is not concerned about our practical lives down here on earth. Stewardship is about your practical earthly life. It is about the choices you make each day. It is about how you spend your money. It is about how you live your life. God wants you to get a revelation of his lordship, and then he wants you to walk in stewardship.

The Lord Has Need of It

> And it come to pass, when he was come nigh to Bethphage and Bethany, at the mount called the mount of Olives, he sent two of his disciples, Saying, Go ye into the village over against you: in the which at your entering ye shall find a colt tied, whereon yet never a man sat: loose him, and bring him hither. And if any man ask you, Why do ye loose him? Thus shall ye say unto him, Because the Lord hath need of him. And they that were sent went their way, and found even as he had said unto them. And as they were loosing the colt, the owners thereof said unto them, Why loose ye the colt? And they said, The Lord hath need of him. (Luke 19:29–34)

There is a stewardship story in the Bible that is often overlooked because of the larger context that it falls in. The larger context is the triumphal entry of Jesus into Jerusalem. Jesus prepares to fulfill the prophecy of his suffering and death by riding into Jerusalem on a colt. As we immerse ourselves into the beginning of the narrative of the passion of Christ, we often don't give much thought to the seemingly simple assignment he gives to his disciples to secure a colt for him to ride on. Jesus sends two of his disciples to retrieve the colt that he will use to ride into the city. The part about stewardship has to do with the owners of the colt. Jesus is aware that there is a man and woman who owns this colt he is sending for. Jesus also knows that the man who owns the colt understands stewardship and sees himself to be a steward of the Lord. Although this colt is in the man's possession, he does not view himself as owning it. He knows that the colt belongs to the Lord. This is stewardship! Jesus continues with his disciples. "And if any man ask you, why do ye loose him? Thus shall ye say unto him, Because the Lord hath need of him" (Luke 19:31). We should note here that when these two disciples arrive at the home, the persons who question their act of loosing the colt are referred to as the "owners" of the colt. "And they that were sent, went their way and found even as he had said unto them. And as they were loosing the colt, the owners thereof said unto them, Why loose ye the colt? And they said, 'The Lord has hath need of him.' And they brought him to Jesus" (Luke 19:32–35). During that day and time, a full-grown colt was a desirable commodity. It had been fed and taken care of by these owners for years. Yet at the simple phrase, "The Lord has need of it," the owners stood down. This passage is inexplicable apart from the understanding of stewardship and lordship. To be a steward is to have possession of the Lord's things. To be a good steward is to have possession of money, cars, resources, or even people at your disposal and hold those things until you hear from the Lord as to whom and how to distribute them. This is the stewardship relationship to the Lord. To be a steward is to have an extra car and to know a friend who needs the car, yet you must seek the Lord as to whether he wants you to give that friend your extra car. Everything a steward owns belongs to the Lord, and a good steward does nothing without consulting the Lord. A certain pastor had been financially blessed by God. He owned several motorcycles. However, he walked in stewardship and under the lordship of Jesus Christ. A friend of his desired to have one of his motorcycles. The man of God said, "Let me pray; and if the Lord agrees, I would be glad to give you one." This is lordship. The Christian who is worldly, carnal, or walking in his intellect will resent such a comment. But a believer who understands stewardship will truly understand that Jesus is Lord and owner of all things. We must not only give; we must give with the intent of doing God's will in our giving. The man of the world gives of his own accord, expecting to receive honor and recognition from men for his giving. The good steward is not content unless he knows that "the Lord has need of it."

Rejection of Lordship

> And as they heard these things, he added and spake a parable, because he was near to Jerusalem, and because they thought that the kingdom of God should immediately appear. (Luke 19:11)

In Luke 19:11–27, Jesus tells a stewardship parable, and the theme of the parable is the rejection of lordship. The parable is prefaced with the mindset of those who are journeying with Jesus. Jesus is approaching Jerusalem, and among the people there is an anticipation of a climax of events. The people who are with him assume that he will do something miraculous and that the kingdom of God will manifest once Jesus reaches Jerusalem. It is against this backdrop that Jesus tells a parable about servants who reject their Lord. These same people who were affirming him at that moment would become oppositional toward him in the near future. There have always been people who invest themselves into Jesus expecting an immediate return on their investment. They desire to join the Christian party at just the right time. Right before the manifestation of the kingdom of God, they are "all in." These types of Christians always end in disappointment. If your faith relies on the spectacular, you will end up among those who have rejected the Lord.

> A certain nobleman went into a far country to receive for himself a kingdom, and to return. And he called his ten servants, and delivered them ten pounds, and said unto them, Occupy until I come. But his citizens hated him and sent message after him, saying, We will not have this man to reign over us. And it came to pass, that when he was returned, having received the kingdom, then he commanded these servants to be called unto him, to whom he had given the money, that he might know how much every man had gained by trading. (Luke 19:12–15)

In chapter 1, I stated that Jesus was not always Lord, but that he became Lord through his obedience and his work on the cross. This parable says that a "certain nobleman went into a far country to receive for himself a kingdom." This nobleman was not a lord and did not possess a kingdom when he left his own country. He made the journey to this far country with hope that he would become lord. However, once he had become the lord, his own citizens decided they did not desire to acknowledge his lordship. So who is this nobleman? It is Jesus. He is telling this parable about himself. We should note that it was not strangers who hated the nobleman, but instead it was "his own citizens." The very people who were espoused to his cause rejected his lordship. This "lord" possessed servants who did not desire that he be lord over their lives. In fact, the text above says that "his citizens hated him." Thus, they rejected lordship. The servants in the story never deny that the main character is their lord. They simply refuse to accept his rulership. This represents the unsurrendered Christian life. It is not a rejection of the salvation of God; it is a rejection of the government of God. There is the unbeliever, and then there is the Christian who refuses to be governed by the Lord Jesus. It is not a Christianity of "I don't desire to be saved." It is a Christianity of "I do not desire to be governed."

Judgment of the Stewards

Nevertheless, the lord of those servants acted magnanimously and gave his servants the resources they would need to advance his kingdom. They were provided money, and they were instructed to "occupy until I come." When the lord of those servants returned, he called for the servants he had given his money to. The parable specifies that there were "ten servants." However, we are apprised of the judgment of only three. The first servant came before his lord and gave an account of faithful stewardship. He had taken his lord's pound and had made ten pounds. The second servant followed with a similar report. He had taken the pound his lord had given him and had made five other pounds. Both of these servants were granted the reward of rulership over cities. The third servant, however, came before his lord with a negative report. He had not gained, nor had he even tried to bring increase to his master. He handed his lord the same pound that was delivered to him. The lord of that servant became angry because his servant had been unproductive. He stripped that servant of even that one pound and delivered it to the servant who produced the ten pounds, leaving him with nothing. The lord of those servants added this refrain, "Unto everyone which hath it shall be given; and from him that hath not, even that he hath shall be taken away" (Luke 19:26). There is a divine reapportionment where the Lord is moving resources from unproductive stewards to productive stewards, causing them to prosper.

> But those mine enemies, which would not that
> I should reign over them, bring hither, and slay
> them before me. (Luke 19:27)

But what of the rest of the citizens who hated the lord? The last line of this parable is one of the oddest references in scripture. The lord of the story called for the execution of his servants. The reference specifically states that the lord demanded the execution of those servants "which did not desire that I reign over them." This represents those who rejected his lordship. Modern men are no different from the servants in this story. The Christianity that is being proffered today is a "lordless Christianity." It is having faith without having a Lord. It is unacceptable to Christ Jesus!

The Unjust Steward

> And he said also unto his disciples, there was a
> certain rich man, which had a steward; and the
> same was accused unto him that he had wasted
> his goods. And he called him, and said to him,
> 'How is it that I hear this of thee? Give an account
> of thy stewardship, for thou mayest be no longer
> steward.' (Luke 16:1–2)

In the book of Luke chapter 16, Jesus tells the story of the unjust steward. It is a story that addresses the matter of financial accountability. As stewards, we are accountable to the Lord Jesus in the management of our finances. Stewardship covers every aspect of our lives, and money does also. The Bible says, "Money answereth all things" (Ecclesiastes 10:19). I can look at your checkbook receipts and tell you both what you value and what things you steward well. In the above parable, the unjust steward had the charge of the rich man's money. The story begins with, "There was a certain rich man which had a steward" (Luke 16:1). The story continues, "The same was accused unto him that he had wasted his goods" (Luke 16:1). The rich man has been told that his steward is wasteful. When you are a steward of the Lord Jesus, you cannot be wasteful. This does not mean that the Lord requires parsimony. However, it does mean that the Lord expects you to be deliberate and responsible in how you manage the things that he has entrusted to you. When a man makes money and then loses it all gambling in the casino, he has wasted his Lord's goods. When a woman is a spendaholic, and she cannot support the kingdom of God because all she receives is immediately spent in stores and in online shopping, she has wasted her Lord's goods. I could give many examples; however, the Holy Spirit will convict you of areas where you are wasteful. The story proceeds with these words, "And he [the lord] called him [the steward], and said unto him, 'How is it that I hear this of thee? Give an account of thy stewardship; for thou mayest be no longer a steward'" (Luke 16:2). The lord of the steward is preparing to tell him, "You're fired!" If the Lord assigns things to you, and you are irresponsible, immoral, negligent, abusive, or wasteful, the Lord will demote you. Many men have prayed that the Lord will bless them with a certain job or public office. But when they entered into that blessing, they squandered it with inappropriate living. Consequently, God took that blessing and gave it to another. As people of God, we need to stop taking God so lightly. Our God is a judge, and he will exact judgment upon those who do not honor him in their living. But you don't have to take my word for it. Consider the word of the Lord to Jeremiah.

> Yea, the stork in the heaven knoweth her appointed times; and the turtle and the crane and the swallow observe the time of their coming; but my people know not the judgment of the Lord. How do ye say, We are wise, and the law of the Lord is with us? Lo, certainly in vain made he it; the pen of the scribe is in vain. The wise men are ashamed, they are dismayed and taken: lo, they have rejected the word of the Lord… Therefore will I give their wives unto others, and their fields to them that shall inherit them; for everyone from the least to the greatest is given to covetousness, from the prophet even to the priest, everyone dealeth falsely. (Jeremiah 8:7–10)

The Lord has not changed. The same Lord that exacted judgment then is officiating your life and your stewardship assignment today. In the parable of the unjust steward, when the lord informed the steward that he was about to lose his stewardship, we are apprised of his inner thoughts. He said to himself, "What shall I do? For my lord taketh away from me the stewardship: I cannot dig; and to beg I am ashamed" (Luke 16:3). The steward even started thinking of the places he could work after he loses his job as steward. Perhaps he could get a job digging ditches. But he had been in this dignified roll of being the king's steward, and digging ditches seemed like a death sentence. The only other option he could think of was to become a beggar. He also realized that he was "ashamed to beg." This was obviously a very difficult spot for the steward. He sat, and he thought. Then suddenly, he had an idea. I know what I will do! The stewardship has not yet been taken from me. I need friends and not a few. "I am resolved what to do, that when I am put out of the stewardship, they may receive me into their houses" (Luke 16:4). Then that steward began to call his lord's debtors and to reduce their bills. By the end of the day, the steward had made quite a few friends. When the lord of that steward called him into judgment, he knew what the steward had done in reducing the people's bills in order to gain friends. You would think he would have been furious about it. However, the lord of that steward was instead rather impressed. "And the lord commended the unjust steward because he had done wisely" (Luke 16:8). If the lord in this story is a type of the Lord Jesus, and the steward in this story is a type of you and I, then what is the meaning of this? The key here is that the lord of the steward told him that he had "done wisely" (Luke 16:8). We should be stewards who understand the power of the wise use of money. We should not just be "spiritually wise"; we must also have the practical wisdom of this world. A good steward is a good money manager. The lord in this story commended the steward because he had managed money to his advantage. Jesus admonished his disciples. "Make to yourselves friends of the mammon of unrighteousness, that when ye fail, they may receive you into everlasting habitations" (Luke 16:9). This simply means that we should help others financially. What did the unjust steward do? He reduced the bills of his lord's debtors, and in so doing, he made friends. If the Lord has blessed you with money, who are you blessing? Who will receive you once your money runs out? This steward was in jeopardy of losing his stewardship. This means that his status was about to change. But while he still held the office of a steward, he acted wisely so as to affect change in his new circumstances. In other words, he used his "current status" as steward to affect his "future status" as jobless. This is the kingdom principle of stewardship at work. A good steward does the work of the Lord on this earth and, consequently, affects his status in heaven. One day, you will be put out of the stewardship of life in a process called death. You will die and no longer be God's steward down here on earth. When you get to heaven, your rewards will be based on the wisdom you used as a steward of God's money and resources down here on earth. No wonder Jesus told this story. He was saying that we all will be put out of the stewardship eventually, and the consequences of our choices while we were stewards will be all that is left.

CHAPTER 7

Fear of the Lord

In its simplest sense, the fear of the Lord means being afraid of God, but not in a panicked sense like the world knows fear. It actually means to reverence God with the understanding that he is almighty and we are mortal. It means to reverence God with the understanding that he is holy and we are sinful. In the Bible, we learned that Job feared God. Job 1:1 says, "There was a man in the land of Uz, whose name was Job; and that man was perfect and upright, and one that feared God, and eschewed evil." Many modern-day Christians give little thought to the matter of fearing God. But Job's fear of the Lord was well noted by the Lord and by the enemy. Job 1:9 says, "Then Satan answered the Lord, and said, Doth Job fear God for nothing?" The fact that Job feared God was on the mind of the enemy, as it was also a defense against the enemy. Ideally, the fear of the Lord should be instilled in us when we are children. As children, we are much more pliable and impressionable than we are as adults. If a child is raised in the fear of the Lord, that reverence for God will remain in him all of his life. But just because one did not learn to fear the Lord as a child does not mean that he cannot learn it as an adult. I was raised by my grandmother. When I was a young boy, when there were thunderstorms, my grandmother would make the children sit down and be still until the storm ceased. She would say, "You all sit still now. The Lord is working." That may sound silly to some intellectuals of today, but it left a profound impression upon us that the Lord was powerful and to be reverenced. The intellectual parent would have instead explained to the children that lightning and thunder are the result of the positive and negative charges in an electric field in the clouds. But this answer would not have generated any fear of the Lord. My grandmother's wisdom and admonition generated in us, at a young age, a profound fear of the Lord. But it was not just the power of the thunderstorms. My grandmother's own reverence for the Lord corroborated her claim and witnessed to us the fear of the Lord as well. While I learned to fear the Lord as a child, there are others who developed a fear of the Lord after being saved as an adult. Your age does not matter; you should learn to fear the Lord. The will of the Lord is done by those who fear him. The Bible says that the fear of the Lord is the beginning of wisdom (Proverbs 9:10). The fear of the Lord is also the beginning of lordship. Therefore, it is understandable that God would favor those believers who genuinely fear him. Psalm 147:11 says, "The Lord takes pleasure in those who fear him."

The Midwives' Fear of God

In the book of Exodus chapter 1, the king of Egypt commanded that all the Hebrew newborn boys were to be killed. The Egyptian king spoke to the Jewish midwives, Shiphrah and Puah, and said, "When you do the office of a midwife to the Hebrew women and see them upon the stools; if it be a son, then ye shall kill him: but if it be a daughter then she shall live" (Exodus 1:15–16). But the king of Egypt did not account for the fact that these Hebrew women feared God. "But the midwives feared God and did not as the king of Egypt commanded them but saved the men children alive" (Exodus 1:17). Notice that it was the midwives' fear of the Lord that made them contradict the king's commandment. There is a blessing in fearing the Lord. Exodus 1:20–21 says, "Therefore, the Lord dealt well with the midwives… And it came to pass, because the midwives feared God, he made them houses." God has always blessed those who fear him.

The fear of the Lord is the beginning of wisdom,
and the knowledge of the holy is understanding.
(Proverbs 9:10)

This verse speaks of both wisdom and knowledge. When you fear the Lord, wisdom is established in your life. The word *wisdom* can be defined as "God's perspective on life." The person who possesses wisdom has the benefit of seeing their circumstances through God's eyes. Big problems look much smaller when you are looking down from the mountaintop of God's perspective. The above verse also speaks of having "knowledge of the holy." This part of the verse is better interpreted as "knowledge of the Holy One." As we fear the Lord, we are established in wisdom. As we gain knowledge about God, we develop understanding about life. If you can begin to have wisdom when you initially fear God, we can extrapolate that to increase in wisdom is to walk continually in the fear of the Lord. The fear of the Lord is not just walking around, hoping God isn't mad at you. Instead, the fear of the Lord is living with an awareness and regard for the Lord's will. Once the fear of the Lord is within you, it will guide you in all you do. Because you fear the Lord, it will place a hedge about you that will not allow the enemy to have access to you. The fear of the Lord exposes the devil! When you walk in the fear the Lord, the deceptions of the devil become apparent in the light of God's presence.

Christ Jesus is the Lord we fear. The manifested God who deals with mankind has always been Christ. In the Old Testament, he manifested himself to them by the name Jehovah, the great God of Israel. Jehovah was the Old Testament preincarnate name for Christ. In the New Testament, the God Jehovah took on a human body and became a man named Jesus. As I stated in chapter 1, Jesus took on a body to save us and to become our Lord. Therefore, to walk under lordship is to fear the Lord Jesus. When the Lord is seeking a man or woman to use for his purposes, he seeks out one who fears him. God brought Moses out of Egypt with the express purpose of using him to deliver his people. If God chose Moses, then Moses must have had the fear of the Lord in him. In the book of Exodus, we find Moses as he was being introduced to God at the burning bush. Exodus 3:6 says, "Moreover he [the Lord] said, I am the God of thy father, the God of Abraham, the God of Isaac, and the God of Jacob. And Moses hid his face, for he was afraid to look upon God." Without the fear of the Lord, Moses would not have qualified to be used by God. The same is true of you.

Manifestations of the Fear of God

> And Jesus went into the temple of God, and cast out all them that sold and brought in the temple, and overthrew the tables of the moneychanger, and the seats of them that sold doves, and said unto them, It is written, My house shall be called the house of prayer; but ye have made it a den of thieves. (Matthew 21:12–13)

In Matthew 21:12–13, Jesus entered the temple and drove out the money changers who were there. These men were using the house of God for their own financial gain. Jesus's expulsion of them represents God's judgment against them. They are being judged because they do not fear God. The temple should have been a place where the presence of God is regarded and respected, but it had become instead just another place to do business. Leviticus 19:30 says, "Ye shall keep my Sabbaths, and reverence my sanctuary: I am the Lord." The fear of the Lord is to respect the presence of God and the things that are dedicated to God. The fear of the Lord can be expressed in many other ways. Your attitude toward the Bible will tell something about your fear of the Lord. Men and women who fear God handle the Scriptures differently from those who do not. Your fear of the Lord is expressed when other people are praying. Those who fear the Lord will have a regard when other people are talking to God. Your fear of the Lord will be expressed through your attitude toward other believers. "As we have therefore opportunity, let us do good unto all men, especially unto them who are of the household of faith" (Galatians 6:10). Your fear of God will even be expressed through your attitude toward the church. If there is no manifested fear of God in your daily life, then you should question the depth of your relationship with the Lord.

The Lord's Anointed

> And he came to the sheepcotes by the way, where there was a cave; and Saul went in to cover his feet: and David and his men remained in the sides of the cave. And the men of David said unto him, Behold the day of which the Lord said unto thee, Behold I will deliver thine enemy into thine hand, that thou may do to him as it may seem good unto thee. Then David arose, and cut off the skirt of Saul's robe privately. And it came to pass afterward, that David's heart smote him, because he had cut off Saul's skirt. And he said unto his men, The Lord forbid that I should do this thing to my master, the Lord's anointed, to stretch forth mine hand against him, seeing he is the anointed of the Lord. (1 Samuel 24:5–6)

Saul had purposed in his heart to kill David without a cause. He had haunted David for years, chasing him through every inch of countryside imaginable. After many years of running from Saul in rank fear, that day had finally come. Saul made the inexplicable error of choosing a bathroom break in the same cave where David and his men were hiding. How amazing was this! David's men immediately recognized it as providence and said, "David, this is your big day! God has delivered your enemy right into your hands, just like he said he would." At that moment, David had the opportunity to drive a dagger right through Saul's heart as he relieved himself in that cave. Despite the admonitions of his men, David restrained himself from harming Saul. It was not because David was afraid to kill, for David was already a man of war. David spared Saul for one reason only. Saul was the Lord's anointed. David's fear of the Lord restrained him on that day. The fear of the Lord is reflected in your respect for those who God has ordained. Because Saul was God's "chosen king" by anointing, David was not willing to kill him even though Saul was unrighteous. Because Saul was the Lord's anointed, he was not to be touched. David regarded what God regarded. David's fear of the Lord was profound. This is lordship!

Sins of Irreverence

> And he [Elisha] went up from thence unto Bethel and as he was going up by the way, there came forth little children out of the city, and mocked him, and said unto him, Go up, thou bald head; go up, thou bald head. And he turned back, and looked on them, and cursed them in the name of the Lord. And there came forth two she bears out of the wood, and tare forty and two children of them. (2 Kings 2:23–24)

To lack respect for ministry and for God's ministers is to lack in the fear of the Lord. In the scripture above, we find children who had not been taught the fear of God. Consequently, these children chose to herald disrespectful and embarrassing comments at the man of God. While Elisha was a man of God, these children didn't regard his status. Because of their impudence, Elisha turned back and cursed them "in the name of the Lord." When he did this, there came forth two she-bears out of the woods and tore forty-two of the children. It should be noted here that Elisha did not choose their punishment. He cursed the children in the name of the one he represented. However, in response to his pronouncement, God chose to send forth two she-bears to discipline these unruly children. The bears were God's choice, and they represented the anger of the Lord toward the children's irreverence. It is also interesting to note that it was two "she bears" that came out against the children. God called forth two mothers from the animal kingdom to discipline human children. The scripture does not say that any of the children were killed; it instead says they were "torn." We could say that God gave these insolent children a severe whipping for their irreverence. When you lose the fear of the Lord, you too will become irreverent.

> And Nadab and Abihu, the sons of Aaron, took each of them his censer, and put fire therein, and put incense thereon, and offered strange fire before the Lord, which he commanded them not. And there went out fire from the Lord, and devoured them, and they died before the Lord. (Leviticus 10:1–2)

In Leviticus 10:1–2, the sons of Aaron, Nadab and Abihu, were the ordained priests serving in the temple. They went ambitiously before the Lord, offering inappropriate sacrifices. They died that day for their indiscretion. At first, their father Aaron was angry with the Lord about the death of his two sons. He talked with Moses about the matter. Moses consoled his bereaved brother concerning the death of his two sons. Moses had these words to say to Aaron, "This is it that the Lord spake, saying, I will be sanctified in them that come near me, and before all the people I will be glorified. And Aaron held his peace" (Leviticus 10:3). Here, we see that God saw Nadab and Abihu's actions as irreverent. They came into the holy temple unwarranted, giving little regard to the presence of the Lord. These two men were lacking in their fear of God, and they died for their irreverence. We must also notice here that God said, "I will be sanctified in those who come near me" (Leviticus 10:3). The word *sanctify* means to be set apart, regarded as holy, and treated with careful reverence. Those who come near the Lord are those who stand in his platform and minister. When a man of God loses careful respect and fear of God, his irreverence is noticed by God. Many pastors and church leaders have died prematurely because they lost their fear of the one they represented. We must remember that irreverent leadership creates irreverent followership, but surrendered leadership creates devoted followership. This is lordship!

> Take the rod, and gather thou the assembly
> together, thou, and Aaron thy brother, and speak
> ye unto the rock before their eyes; and it shall
> give forth his water. (Numbers 20:8)

> And Moses and Aaron gathered the congregation
> together before the rock, and he said unto them,
> Hear now ye rebels; must we fetch you water out
> of this rock? And Moses lifted up hand, and with
> his rod he struck the rock twice: and water come
> out abundantly, and the congregation drank, and
> their beasts also. (Numbers 20:10–11)

Moses also made a similar error of irreverence. In the book of Numbers, while the children of Israel journeyed through the wilderness, the people needed water. The people became angry and agitated with both God and Moses because of the lack of water. God was obliged to give the people water. He gave instruction to Moses as to how he wanted to give water to his people. Moses was to gather the people into an assembly before the great rock that was there in the wilderness. However, by the time of the assembly, the people had angered Moses. At the assembly, Moses's anger boiled over, and instead of "speaking" to the rock as God had commanded him, Moses instead struck the rock. In our minds, this would seem like it is no big deal, only a slight change in the program by Moses. But to God it was an act of irreverence. Moses was not careful to sanctify the Lord before the people. Because of this one act, Moses was not allowed to enter the promised land, a dream he had looked forward to for forty years. "And the Lord spake unto Moses and Aaron, Because ye believed me not, to sanctify me in the eyes of the children of Israel, therefore ye shall not bring this congregation into the land which I have given them" (Numbers 20:12). I am sure this statement was deflating to Moses. The lesson in this is that God must be glorified in all that we do. "Whether therefore ye eat, or drink, or whatever ye do, do all to the glory of God" (1 Corinthians 10:31). If you are in ministry, and you have become angry or irreverent, you need to step aside. You are likely to do damage to yourself, to God's people, or to God's reputation. Because of his anger, Moses lost his reverence for God that day at the rock, and he paid a precious price for it. The Lord is glorified by our reverence and defamed by our irreverence.

> But a certain man named Ananias, with Sapphira his wife, sold a possession, and kept back part of the price, his wife being privy to it, and brought a certain part, and laid it at the apostles' feet. But Peter said, Ananias, why hath Satan filled thine heart to lie to the Holy Ghost, and to keep back part of the price of the land…why have thou conceived this thing in thine heart? Thou have not lied unto men, but unto God. And Ananias hearing these words fell down, and gave up the ghost. (Acts 5:1–5)

Do you know the story of Ananias and Sapphira? At Pentecost, God introduced the Holy Spirit into the life of the early church. The Holy Spirit is the attendant third member of the Godhead. He is the very manifestation of God being with us and the seal of our salvation. From Pentecost forward, the church had witnessed the manifestation of the Holy Spirit, miracles, and great power. Consequently, many of the saints wanted to support this cause financially. Many of them sold their possessions and made prolific financial contributions to advance the work of the Lord. Ananias and Sapphira were two married believers who were there in the young church. They too sold their personal property but kept back a part of the proceeds from the sale. They then brought the remaining sum of money to Apostle Peter, presenting it to him as the full amount of the sale price. The issue at hand was not the selling of the property. It was their property, and they were not forced to sell it. The issue here is not a need for more money for the church. The salient issue here was the fact that they introduced deception in the presence of God the Holy Spirit! God deemed the act as irreverence toward the Holy Spirit. Lying to the Holy Spirit is disrespect for God's omniscience and holiness. Since the Holy Spirit is "the Spirit of the Lord," then this act is a reflection of their lack of fear of the Lord. "But Peter said, Ananias, why hath Satan filled thine heart to lie to the Holy Ghost, and keep back part of the price of the land…thou has not lied unto men, but unto God." Ananias and Sapphira both died that day for their indiscretion. Their lack of fear and reverence for the presence of the Holy Spirit cost them their lives. In this age of disrespect toward everything, we would do well to grow in our fear of God. While the world grows more disrespectful and irreverent, we as believers should be increasing in our determination to walk in the fear of the Lord. This is lordship!

Three Errors of the Babylonians

In 2 Kings chapter 17, God allowed the Assyrians to have victory over the Israelites in war, and they carried the Israelites away as captives of war. Then the king of Assyria supplanted the Israelite cities of Samaria with Babylonians. When the Babylonians came to live in Samaria, a blatant problem arose. The Babylonians were in the place of God's people, but they lacked knowledge of the God of the land. These Babylonians made an effort to comply with the God of the Israelites but unsuccessfully. The Babylonians erred in three ways.

Error 1: They lacked the fear of God.

> And the king of Assyria brought men from Babylon and from Cuthah, and from Ava and from Hamath and from Sepharvaim, and placed them in the cities of Samaria instead of the Children of Israel: and they possessed Samaria, and dwelt in the cities thereof. And so it was at the beginning of their dwelling there, that they feared not the Lord: Therefore, the Lord sent lions among them, which slew some of them. Wherefore, they spake to the king of Assyria, saying, the nations which thou hast removed,

and placed in the cities of Samaria, know not the manner of the God of the land: therefore he hath sent lions among them and behold they slay them, because they know not the manner of the God of the Land. (2 Kings 17:24–26)

We can see that the Babylonians were totally oblivious to the fact that they should fear God. God punished them for their error, sending ravenous lions among them. But this is not only back then. There are Christians today who are walking under lionlike curses because they are lacking in the fear of the Lord. This text says that these Babylonians "did not know the manner of God." The manner of a servant of the Lord is that he walks in the fear of the Lord.

Error 2: They feared God but served idols.

Then the king of Assyria commanded saying, Carry thither one of the priests whom ye brought from thence, and let them go and dwell there, and let him teach them [the Babylonians] the manner of the God of the land. Then one of the priests whom they carried away from Samaria came and dwelt in Bethel and taught them how they should fear the Lord. Howbeit every nation made gods of their own and put them in the houses of the high places which the Samaritans had made, every nation in their cities wherein thy dwelt… So they feared the Lord, and made unto themselves of the lowest of them priest of the high places, which sacrificed for them in their houses of the high places. They feared the Lord and served their own gods, after the manner of the nations whom they carried away from thence. (2 King 17:27–33)

The king of Assyria responded wisely, calling for one of the Israelite priests to come and teach the Babylonians how to fear God. However, once the Babylonians got wind of the importance of fearing God, they made another error. They began to trend toward being religious, and they had regard for every god. They made the lowest of men priest to serve in the high places and to assist them in their religious practices. Their "fear" was not reserved for God alone. This represents the man who will say "amen" when you are speaking of the Lord Jesus. He is just as enthusiastic when people are speaking of other religions. Like the Babylonians, his fear is not limited to Christ alone!

Error 3: The fear of other gods

> Unto this day they do after the former manners: they fear not the Lord, neither do they after their statues, or after their ordinances, or after the law and commandment which the Lord commanded the children of Jacob, whom he named Israel. With whom the Lord had made a covenant, and charged them, saying, Ye shall not fear other gods, nor bow yourselves to them, nor serve them, nor sacrifice to them: But the Lord, who brought you up out of the land of Egypt with great power and a stretched out arm, him shall ye fear, and him shall ye worship, and to him shall ye do sacrifice. And the statues and ordinances, and the law, and commandments, which he wrote for you, ye shall observe to do for evermore, and ye shall not fear other gods. And the covenant that I have made with you ye shall not forget: neither shall ye fear other gods. But the Lord your God ye shall fear: and he shall deliver you out of the hand of all your enemies. Howbeit they did not hearken, but they did after their former manner. So these nations feared the Lord and served their graven images, both their children, and their children's

> children: as did their fathers, so do they unto this
> day. (2 Kings 17:34–41)

The Babylonians developed a fear of every god. Their fear of the gods drove their frenzied religious practices. When a person has fear of any god besides the Lord, it brings an error and a snare. To fear other gods is just as forbidden with the Lord as failing to fear him. When a person fears other gods, they are saying essentially that the Lord is not the only God. They are saying that the Lord cannot protect them. The belief in superstition is fear of other gods. Respect for the occult is to fear other gods. To practice witchcraft is to fear other gods. There are many people who claim the banner of Christianity, who also do these things.

Fear of the Lord Is Wisdom

The Bible says that the fear of the Lord is wisdom (Proverbs 9:10). Any believer who wants to be counted as wise must begin with a determination to properly fear God. There are blessings that are directly ascribed to those who fear God. Malachi 4:2 says, "But unto you that fear my name shall the Sun of righteousness arise with healing in his wings; and ye shall go forth, and grow up as calves of the stall." These blessings of healing and prosperity are promised directly to those who fear the Lord. I have heard Isaiah 59:19 partially quoted on many occasions. However, when you hear the entire verse, you realize it is a promise to those who fear the Lord. "So shall they fear the name of the Lord from the west, and his glory from the rising of the sun. When the enemy shall come in like a flood, the Spirit of the Lord shall lift up a standard against him" (Isaiah 59:19). There is yet another scripture in Jeremiah where God is expressing his amazement that men do not recognize him and fear him.

> Fear ye not me? saith the Lord: will ye not tremble
> at my presence, which have placed the sand for
> the bound of the sea by a perpetual degree, that it
> cannot pass it: and though the waves thereof toss

themselves yet can they not prevail; though they roar, yet can they not pass over it. But his people hath a revolting and a rebellious heart; they are revolted and gone. Neither say they in their heart, Let us now fear the Lord our God, that giveth rain, both the former and the latter, in his season: he reserves unto us the appointed weeks of harvest. (Jeremiah 5:22–24)

This verse is saying that we should fear God simply because of our dependency upon him for provision. If we are lacking wisdom, then we are simply lacking in the fear of the Lord.

CHAPTER 8

Pleasing the Lord

There are many people who claim the title of "Christian." However, the believer who is under lordship is far less interested in claiming he is a Christian for social reasons and far more interested in pleasing the Lord. While many Christians pride themselves that they are "God-conscious," many of them are living their lives with no knowledge or awareness of God's opinion of themselves. Contrarily, lordship asks daily, "What does the Lord think of this or that?" Lordship asks incessantly, "What does the Lord think of my ways, my thoughts, or my deeds?" Embracing lordship is an inner desire to please the Lord. Those who are bound by this world always seek the acceptance and acknowledgment of men. But those who are under lordship are set to do whatever it takes to receive God's approval. There is a pulling of the world to draw the believer into a life of men-pleasing. Men-pleasing is when a person honors men above their honor for God. Men-pleasing is the desire for acceptance, acknowledgment, and recognition from men that causes the believer to distance himself from the Lord. Galatians 1:10 says, "For do I now persuade men, or God? Or do I seek to please men? For if I yet please men, I should not be the servant of Christ." This scripture states that if a person seeks to please men, then his status as a servant of the Lord is suspended. Jesus said, "How can ye believe, which receive honor one of another, and seek not the honor that comes from God alone?"

(John 5:44). You were created to please God. When you are under lordship, pleasing the Lord is your mission and your goal. Salvation comes to the individual who realizes that the sins of his past life were not pleasing to the Lord. As he comes into that realization, he sees his need for the mercy and forgiveness offered through the Lord Jesus Christ. Once he is saved, his future life has a new agenda and that is pleasing the Lord. Modern-day Christianity has drifted so far away from the standards of God. Many modern-day believers erroneously believe that it is God's job to please them. Many are even angry that God is not doing a good enough job at pleasing them. But those believers who are under lordship know that all things must be done to please the Lord.

How does the believer please the Lord? I am glad you asked! The Bible has much to say about the prospect of pleasing the Lord. Consider the simple matter of faith. When a person simply believes the Lord, it is pleasing to the Lord. Hebrews 11:6 says, "But without faith it is impossible to please him; for he that comes to God must believe that he is, and that he is a rewarder of them that diligently seek him." Thus, we could conclude that one of the ways we please God is simply by believing his word. Hebrews 11:5 testifies of Enoch's faith, saying that "before he was translated, he had this testimony, that he pleased God." The Bible also teaches us that our worship pleases the Lord. Psalm 69:30–31 says, "I will praise the name of God with a song and will magnify him with thanksgiving. This also shall please the Lord better than an ox or bullock that hath horns and hoofs." There are also many other scriptures that tell us that God is pleased with our worship. The primary purpose of the believer's life must be to please the Lord. Apostle Paul wrote many references that directly addressed pleasing the Lord. 1 Thessalonians 4:1 says, "Furthermore, then we beseech you brethren, and exhort you by the Lord Jesus, that as ye have received of us how ye ought to walk and to please God, so ye would abound more and more." This epistle is exhorting us that we should be progressively improving at pleasing God. The Bible also declares many instances where God is contrarily displeased. Speaking of the Israelites in the wilderness, the apostle of First Corinthians narrates the things God did for the people in the wilderness, but then he writes, "But with many of them God was not well pleased: for they were overthrown in the wilderness" (1 Corinthians 10:5). Then there is God's servant David who killed Uriah and took Uriah's wife Bathsheba for himself. Concerning these things, 2 Samuel 11:27 records, "But the thing that David had done displeased the Lord." There are many believers today who are being chastised by the Lord because their lives, their choices, their attitudes, their manners are not pleasing to the Lord. Everything the believer does is being recorded, and he shall give an account of it in the judgment. Our goal is to be, in every way, like our Lord Jesus. The Father testified of his life, "And lo a voice from heaven, saying, This is my beloved Son, in whom I am well pleased" (Matthew 3:17).

Walking Worthy of the Calling

> For this cause we also, since the day we heard it, do not cease to pray for you, and to desire that ye might be filled with the knowledge of his will, in all wisdom and spiritual understanding; that ye might **walk worthy of the Lord unto all pleasing**, being fruitful in every good work, and increasing in the knowledge of God. (Colossians 1:9–10, emphasis added)

Another way the New Testament exhorts the believer in the matter of pleasing the Lord is by the expression "Walk worthy of the call." The New Testament use of the word *walk* does not refer to taking physical steps to move forward but instead is referencing ones "manner of life." This phrase "walking worthy of the call" simply means to render back to God a devoted and sanctified life for the salvation he has afforded you. When the apostle Paul heard that there were new believers in Colosse he immediately assayed to write to them and encourage them in their faith. The above section of scripture is the record of Paul's prayer for the new believers in Colossae. When reading it, you can sense Paul's sincere concern for the new believers. He expressed many aspects of the faith that were important for them to embrace and receive. A portion of the apostle's exhortation was that they should "walk worthy of the Lord unto all pleasing." Another way this could be expressed is "see that ye aspire in every way to please the Lord." A person's salvation should be evidenced by the manner in which he lives his life. This reference implies holiness to God and evidence to man. God should know that you live a holy life and man should see the evidence of that consecrated life. On another occasion, Apostle Paul addressed the same matter with the believers in Rome with these words, "I beseech you therefore, brethren, by the mercies of God, that ye present your bodies a living sacrifice, holy, acceptable unto God, which is your reasonable service. And be not conformed to this world: but be ye transformed by the renewing of your mind" (Romans 12:1–2). The believer who does not chasten his lifestyle has forgotten what great price God paid to secure his salvation.

Sexual Purity

> Furthermore, then we beseech you brethren, and exhort you by the Lord Jesus, that as ye have received of us how **ye ought to walk and to please God**, so ye would abound more and more. For ye know what commandments we gave you by the Lord Jesus. For this is the will of God, even your sanctification; that ye should abstain from fornication *[sexual immorality]*: That every one of you should know how to possess his vessel *[body]* in sanctification and honor. Not in the lust of concupiscence *[strong sexual desire]*, even as the Gentiles *[unsaved]* which know not God... For God has not called us to uncleanness but to holiness. (1 Thessalonians 4:1–7, emphasis added)

The Lord Jesus calls every born-again believer to live a holy life. The believer who is under lordship accepts God's call to holiness as his Christian responsibility. If a believer disregards the Lord's call to holiness, his life will drift away from lordship. I cannot overemphasize this point. Many believers who at one time in their life enjoyed a close walk with the Lord are now wondering in a mental wilderness, incarcerated in prison, or even dead because they abdicated the responsibility to live a holy life. Holy living is Christian responsibility 101. Holy living reinforces the fear of God in the believer, and the fear of God reinforces holiness. Many believers today desire to "do great things for God." But the Word of God speaks clearly to us that if we simply live a holy life, we will not miss out on anything the Lord has for us. There is no need to search for a "great work to do for the Lord." Today's "great work" for the believer should be to be a good representative for the Lord, allowing others to see Jesus in you through the consecrated and sanctified life that you live. This is lordship!

The scripture above tells us that holy living pleases the Lord. It also speaks specifically of the matter of "possessing your vessel." Your body is the "vessel" that is being referenced in that scripture. Everyone possesses a physical body. After you are born again, your assignment from God is for you to master your vessel (body) with its desires and proclivities. Second Corinthians 7:1 says, "Having therefore these promises, dearly beloved, let us cleanse ourselves from all filthiness of flesh and spirit, perfecting holiness in the fear of God." There are the natural desires of the body such as food, sleep, sex, and the like. When the believer has possession of himself, he has these things under control. He does not overeat. He is not lazy. He does not participate in the sexual immorality of this world. He has his "appetites" under control. This is pleasing to God! God knows that the sex drive is a particularly challenging thing, and thus, he has provided marriage as a resolution to this matter. 1 Corinthians 7:2 says, "Nevertheless, to avoid sexual immorality, let every man have his own wife, and let every woman have her own husband." It is God's divine will and purpose that the believer embrace marriage. While we all must experience being single for a season of our lives, to be perpetually single can be a satanic weapon and assignment that has been launched against the believer. The enemy wants the believer single and seeking to resolve their sexual desires in a promiscuous world.

This state creates many challenges for the saint and many opportunities for the enemy. Many believers need to resolve in their hearts that God's purpose for their life is that they become a marriageable man or woman. It is God's will for the believer to marry first and then engage in sexual relationship after marriage. This is God's standard of holiness. We live in a world that is sexually saturated with promiscuity and does not regard the Lord's will in sexual matters. However, the believer who is under lordship does. The believer who is beset by sexual urges must seek the Lord for the companionship of marriage. The married believer must grow in character so as to have the consistency needed to maintain a positive marital relationship. This is lordship.

> Now the works of the flesh and manifested, which are these; Adultery *[Sexual relationship with any person who is married to another person]*, fornication *[sexual immorality: incest, prostitution, masturbation, orgies, bestiality, pornography, etc.]*, uncleanness *[homosexuality]*, lasciviousness *[sexually lewd or provocative]*, idolatry *[worship of idols]*, witchcraft *[casting spells]*, hatred *[extreme dislike]*, variance *[to teach falsely]*, emulations *[excessive desire for success]*, wrath *[uncontrolled anger]*, strife *[conflicts between individuals]*, seditions *[resistance to lawful authority]*, heresies *[false teaching]*, envying *[extreme jealousy]*, murders *[to kill]*, drunkenness *[alcoholism]*, reveling *[wild parties]*, and such like: of the which I tell you before, as I have also told you in time past, that they which do such things shall not inherit the kingdom of God. (Galatians 5:19–21)

In addition to having natural appetites and drives that derive from our bodies, we also have the sinful Adamic nature. While our natural bodies are demanding food, water, clothing, sex, sleep, and so forth, the sinful nature within us is making its demand on us also. Being born again does not completely cancel the sinful nature in us because until we die and go to heaven, we still possess these unredeemed Adamic bodies. The sinful nature is manifested in us through our bodies. Our fleshly bodies may make demands for any of the sins that are listed above: adultery, fornication, uncleanness, and so forth. The manifestation of these things in us makes us ungodly and unholy. The Bible refers to these sinful drives within us as "the works of the flesh." As long as we are in the flesh, we will be at war with our flesh. Thus, the believer must battle the devil while simultaneously battling himself. This is what the apostle Paul was speaking of when he said, "But I keep under my body, and bring it into subjection: lest that by any means, when I have preached to others, I myself should be a castaway" (1 Corinthians 9:27). To be under lordship is to walk in the stewardship of your body as you serve the Lord with your living.

> But fornication, and all uncleanness *[homosexuality or bestiality]*, or covetousness *[excessive desire for things]*, let it not be once named among you as becometh saints: Neither filthiness *[morally offensive or obscene]*, nor foolish talking *[unholy conversation]*, nor jesting *[sexually explicit or inappropriate comments or joking]*, which are not convenient: but rather giving of thanks. For this ye know, that no whoremonger, nor unclean person, nor covetous man, who is an idolater, hath any inheritance in the kingdom of Christ and of God. Let no man deceive you with vain words: for because of these things cometh the wrath of God upon the children of disobedience. Be not ye therefore partakers with them. (Ephesians 5:3–7)

The word *fornication* is from the Greek word *porneia*. This word is the root of our word *pornography*. When the modern mind thinks of pornography, we think of viewing sexual acts. However, to be biblically clear, pornography is viewing sexual immorality or what the

Bible calls fornication. *Uncleanness* is a word that is associated with homosexuality. Because God created the natural attraction between a man and a woman, the word *uncleanness* would imply any sexual act that is "unnatural." This includes both homosexuality and bestiality also. In Romans 1:22–28, the Bible is speaking explicitly about people who were inclined to homosexuality. Romans 1:24 specifically says, "God gave them over to uncleanness." This means that God withdrew his grace that keeps us and allowed them to trend toward unnatural sexual acts. The believer who has homosexual desires is not exempt from the responsibility of living a holy life. Our modern society has placed homosexuality in a special class as if it is a lifestyle choice. However, in scripture, we see that it is listed right along with adultery and fornication. Homosexuality is just another manifestation of the Adamic nature within the body. The homosexual person must be cleansed from his iniquity by the power of the Lord Jesus Christ just as others. If the believer would take up the responsibility to oppose the sinful inclinations of his flesh, the Lord Jesus will assist him to victory, and his life will be pleasing to the Lord.

A Great House

> But in a great house, there are not only vessels
> of gold and of silver, but also of wood and earth;
> and some to honor and some to dishonor. If a
> man therefore purge himself from these, he shall
> be a vessel unto honor sanctified and meet for the
> master's use, and prepared unto every good work.
> (2 Timothy 2:20–21)

When you became born-again, you were placed in God's great house. The Lord's house as referenced in the scripture above is his kingdom. We are those "vessels" that are within the house. The scripture above draws on the analogy of a house to help us to see something important about our service to the Lord. When you enter into a rich man's house, there are many "vessels" he uses to do many different things. There are vessels that are used to wash dirty shoes, and there are vessels he uses to serve dignitaries. These vessels all differ in their purpose as they also differ in their makeup. Gold and silver vessels are not used for the same purposes as wood and clay vessels. In the kingdom of God, the Lord does not consign us to be gold, silver, wood, or clay. This consignment is the result of our own dedication and consecration to the Lord. If the servant of the Lord purges himself from sexual immorality and separates himself from ungodly practices, he will be used for greater purposes from the Lord. If the believer is content to live an unsanctified life, then the assignments and purposes that God calls him to and uses him for will reflect a lower grade. The promise from the Lord here is that if the servant of the Lord cleanses himself from unrighteousness, the Lord will honor his sanctification.

Expanding Our View of Holiness

> This I say therefore, and testify in the Lord, that ye henceforth walk not as other Gentiles walk in the vanity of their own mind. Having the understanding darkened, being alienated from the life of God through the ignorance that is in them because of the blindness of their hearts. (Ephesians 4:17–18)

Often when we speak of God's call to holiness, we immediately think of sexual purity. However, walking in holiness is not just sexual purity. Ephesians chapters 4–5 speak of many other types of unholiness such as greed, lying, anger, pride, stealing, laziness, corrupt communication, bitterness, wrath, malice, gossip, unthankfulness, covetousness, and the like. The call to holiness expands beyond sexuality. The believer must be cleansed from all these unrighteous things so that his life will please God. Living under lordship and pleasing the Lord means eliminating excesses. There are some things that are lawful for the believer to do, but if done in excess, they contend against lordship. Things like television, sports, news, work, dining, travel, even things that are done to make money legally are all lawful for us to do but should not be done in excess. When your life pleases the Lord, Christ will confer divine favor upon you. This favor from God brings prosperity and facilitates God's will for your life.

CHAPTER 9

Worship the Lord

Worship is the private and public practice of honoring the Lord. The truest test as to whether Jesus Christ is Lord over your life is that you worship him. If you follow every principle that I have taught in this book, but you do not worship Christ, then he is not Lord over your life. The very concept of "Lord" demands worship. The word *Lord* actually means "the one whom I worship and obey." To reject worship is to reject lordship. Worship is the one indisputable, undeniable, and indispensable thing that propels you into a lordship relationship with Christ. Worship is also a part of our earthly assignment. You were created to worship God; therefore, worship is not optional. When I say worship, I am not advocating attending a certain type of church. To walk under lordship is to worship the Lord publicly as well as privately. The church you attend is only relevant in the sense that it should assist you in the practice of public worship. It is interesting to note that in all churches, no matter their denomination, their public gatherings are called Worship Services although in some churches, there is not much worship of the Lord taking place. To embrace the kingdom and to walk under Christ's lordship, you must stay mindful of the fact that Jesus did not start a denomination. Christ redeemed us by his own blood. Therefore, Christ's kingdom is the believer's only denomination. To walk under lordship is to fully embrace both the public and private worship of God. Being a part of a public worship experience is important, and there are many benefits. However, when I speak of worship here in this chapter, I am primarily speaking of personal worship. To walk in a revelation of lordship is to embrace and develop a personal worship relationship to God the Father and to the Lord Jesus Christ.

What Is God's Value to You?

Worship is the spontaneous response to something or someone a person highly values. What you worship is simply what you value the most. If one does not worship God, one simply does not value God properly. Much of the mentoring of God and the development of our personal testimony has to do with the believer learning to value God more. For some people, God is simply a resort that they turn to when they are in trouble. However, this is not the proper value that God is looking for. God is looking for sons and daughters who value him more than life itself. Romans 1:21 is an interesting description of a group of people who knew God but did not value God. "Because that when they knew God, they glorified him not as God, neither were thankful: but became vain in their imaginations, and their foolish hearts were darkened." This is not a group that is described as people who "did not know God." The group in this scripture are described as people who "knew God" but failed to value God properly, and consequently, they did not worship God. They worshipped, but it was not God. What did they worship? "They worshipped and served the creature [man] more than the Creator, who is blessed forever" (Romans 1:25). If a person is lacking in the proper value he ascribes to God, that person will also be lacking in the proper worship of God.

> And David danced before the Lord with all
> his might: and David was girded with a linen
> ephod… And as the Ark of the Lord came into
> the city of David, Michal Saul's daughter looked
> through a window, and saw king David leaping

and dancing before the Lord; and she despised
him in her heart. (2 Samuel 6:14–16)

In the scripture above, David danced before the Lord with all his might. David danced as an act of worship to God to show his appreciation for the long-awaited return of the ark of the covenant. The ark was the tabernacle of God and in it dwelled the manifested presence of God. It was important to David to know that God was with him. David's value of God was great. His wife Michal, however, disapproved of David's public show of worship, and she despised him for it. Too often it is this matter of worship that separates the believers from the Christians. David's wife was trying to make David accept her lower estimation of God's importance. She said to David, "You really made yourself look bad out there dancing in front of all those people today" (2 Samuel 6:20, paraphrased). David renounced her estimation of his actions and her valuation of God. He said to her, "God has made me to be king and appointed me to be ruler over his people Israel. And I will be humble before Him and place value on God and not on myself!" (2 Samuel 6:21–22, paraphrased) Other Bible scholars suggest that Michal wanted David to maintain his sense of dignity as being royalty. David's wife relished the status and titles associated with being part of the royal family. She was a dignified woman. Dignity is defined as the state of being worthy of honor or respect. Human dignity has to do with the measure of the value you place on yourself. The need to be dignified is a hindrance to the worship of God. Many Christians do not worship God because the worship of God is a detraction of their own sense of dignity. God is not glorified in the lives of many Christians who seek to maintain a sense of dignity. We will not reach beyond ourselves and open our mouths in profuse praise and worship until the idol of human dignity is cast down.

Acts of Worship

There are many biblical expressions of worship such as clapping the hands, dancing, raising the hands, singing, shouting, giving of offering, and the like. All these are mentioned in scripture, and any of these acts can be used in your time of personal worship. While these biblical expressions of worship are often used by believers, it does not preclude anyone from making up their own improvised "acts of worship." One woman would go to her church and lie on the floor, prostrate before the Lord, to show her appreciation for all he had done for her. It was her personal act of worship, and it is acceptable to the Lord. As you develop a personal worship unto the Lord, you will use both biblical and personal acts of worship in your worship of God.

Thanksgiving, Praise, and Worship

There are three primary categories of worship. They are thanksgiving, praise, and adoration. Thanksgiving is a verbal expression of gratitude and appreciation of someone who believes God has done something for him. Thanksgiving is also rehearsing the historical goodness and benevolence of God. The word *praise* means "to magnify." Praise is celebrating the acts of God on earth through words or song. Adoration (worship) is the esteeming of God's character. To worship means to express a high degree of personal reverence or veneration to God for who he is. Any of these acts of worship can be done vocally as well as done silently in one's heart. It is important that we grow to learn to distinguish these three expressions. As a general rule, we worship God for who he is (character), and we praise him for what he does (acts). We should be deliberate in our intention to offer God all three of these acts of worship. We should also be intentional to worship God vocally and publicly whenever it is appropriate. There are different occasions that call for each of these three expressions, and there are different scriptures that teach us about each one. Hebrews 13:15 teaches us simultaneously about praise and thanksgiving saying, "By him therefore, let us offer the sacrifice of praise to God continually, that is, the fruit of our lips giving thanks to his name." Psalm 150:6 advocates praise saying, "Let everything that has breath praise the Lord." Everything that has breath includes you. The Bible reports that God is due worship from every creature on this plant. Nothing or no one is excluded. It does not omit the affluent, or the intelligent, or the sophisticated. Everything that has breath means everyone. Psalm 86:9 speaks of worship and says, "All nations whom thou has made shall come and worship before thee, O Lord: and shall glorify thy name." Worship gets the attention of God. It is the one thing that he is attracted to. But more importantly, it is the thing he deserves from you. In Luke chapter 17, Jesus healed ten lepers by sending them to see the priest before there was any manifestation of their healing. As they journeyed to see the priest, they were all healed. One of the men, when he recognized he had been healed, went back to Jesus to offer to him praise and adoration for this healing benefit. When Jesus saw the man worshipping, he said, "Were there not ten cleansed? But where are the nine? There are not found that returned to give glory to God except this stranger" (Luke 17:17–18). Jesus's expectation was that all those men who were healed would give glory to God for their healing. His expectations have not changed. When men receive the benefits of God, their responsibility is to return glory to God for all he has done. David wrote, "What shall I render unto the Lord for all his benefits toward me?" (Psalm 116:12) For all that God has done in your life, your best rendering back to the Lord is your worship, praise, and thanksgiving! The Father is seeking men and women who when he gives them his blessings, they will offer back to him their worship.

The Woman at the Well

> The woman saith unto him, Sir I perceive that thou art a prophet. Our fathers worshipped in this mountain; and ye say that in Jerusalem is the place where men ought to worship. Jesus saith unto her, Woman, believe me, the hour cometh, when ye shall neither in this mountain, nor yet at Jerusalem, worship the Father. Ye worship ye know not what: we know what we worship: for salvation is of the Jews. But the hour cometh, and

> now is, when the true worshippers shall worship
> the father in spirit and in truth: for the Father
> seeketh such to worship him. God is a Spirit:
> and they that worship him must worship him in
> spirit and in truth. (John 4:19–24)

Worship is intimacy with God. Just as a man and a woman have intimacy together, so does one have intimacy with God, just not in a sexual manner. Intimacy with God is spiritual. It is a matter of believing that God has a perfect heart for you, just as you are developing a perfect heart toward him. The lordship relationship is one of intimacy and instruction. Jesus mentors us as we worship him. In the passage above, Jesus initiated a conversation with a Samaritan woman. It did not take the woman long to realize she was talking with someone who was special. She said to him, "Sir, I perceive that you are a prophet" (John 4:19). She turned the conversation immediately to the matter of the place of worship. During biblical times, there was a theological belief that God was in a certain place or preferred certain places. Therefore, they built tabernacles and temples in every place where there was a manifestation of God. The woman asked Jesus which group was correct in their place of worship, the Samaritans or the Jews. Jesus unapologetically instructed her, explaining to her that not only were the Jews correct but that the worship of the Samaritans was not even directed at God. Then Jesus informed her that locating the proper place of worship shall no longer be an issue. The issue at this point is knowing that the place of worship that God prefers are the spirits of men. We are the temples that God longs to dwell in and receive worship from. God is looking for true worshippers that will worship him in spirit and in truth.

We are tripartite beings. That simply means that we have three parts. There is our outer self, which is our fleshly body, and there is our inner self, which is our spirit man. The third part is the soul, which consists of the mind, the will, and the emotions. The soul of a man resides somewhere between the body and the spirit. A religious person seeks to worship God from his outer self. This would include his mind and his body working together in doing religious acts. There are many religious people who do not know God but perform outward acts of worship. However, there is the inner self or the spirit man. This is the part of us that was regenerated when we became born-again. It is within the inner self or spirit man where the Holy Spirit dwells. This is the place where true worship happens. Your flesh does not incline to worship God. The flesh that we live in is sinful and has not been redeemed; it will return to dust. It is our inner man, our spirit man, which desires to worship and praise God—and not our flesh. This means that our outer man or natural man opposes what our inner man or spirit man desires. "But the natural man receives not the thing of the spirit of God: for they are foolishness unto him" (1 Corinthians 2:14). The Father is seeking men and women who will worship him from within their recreated spirit. Those who have learned to worship have learned to live from their inner man, from their spirit man. The believer who has tapped into his spirit man will find worship to be the well of water that blesses God and refreshes his soul.

The War for Worship

> How art thou fallen from heaven, O Lucifer, son of the morning! How art thou cut down to the ground, which didst weaken the nations! For thou hast said in thine heart, I will ascend into heaven, I will exalt my throne above the stars of God: I will sit also upon the mount of the congregation, in the sides of the north: I will ascend above the heights of the clouds; I will be like the Most High. Yet thou shalt be brought down to hell, to the sides of the pit. (Isaiah 14:12–15)

There is an invisible battle going on in the earth. This battle is for the worship of men. From the very beginning, we find that Satan desired to wrest worship from the Father. In Isaiah 14, we are told of his rebellion in heaven. The downfall of Lucifer was his desire to be worshipped. Has anything changed about our enemy? Consider his words to Jesus in the book of Matthew, "Again the devil taketh him up into an exceeding high mountain, and sheweth him all the kingdoms of the world, and the glory of them. And saith unto him, All these things will I give thee if thou will fall down and worship me" (Matthew 4:8–9). We can easily see that the devil has not changed; he still seeks to steal the worship of God. If Satan is seeking worshippers, and God the Father is seeking worshippers, we can easily see the true source of the spiritual battle. The real question becomes who, or what, are you worshipping? Are you worshipping the Father; or have you become like Satan, saying, "I too will be worshipped"? There are also mortal men who are standing in the principle of Satan because they too desire to be worshipped. There is a war going on over worship. Christians who feel that worship is optional, or unnecessary, do not understand the great battle that is waging over the worship of men.

Many of us have heard of the story of Shadrach, Meshach, and Abednego. In Daniel chapter 3, we see how Satan used the Babylonian king Nebuchadnezzar to force the Jewish people to worship an idol statue. Nebuchadnezzar made a large statue. Afterward, he gave this commandment:

> To you it is commanded, O people, nations and languages, that at what time ye hear the sound of the cornet, flute, harp, sackbut, psaltery, dulcimer, and all kinds of music, ye fall down and worship the golden image that Nebuchadnezzar the king has set up: And whoso falleth not down and worship shall the same hour be cast into the midst of a burning fiery furnace. (Daniel 3:4–6)

This story is not the expression of a misguided king. Behind every earthly act of worship, someone or something is glorified. Believers need to take worship much more seriously. King Nebuchadnezzar was being used by Satan to redirect the worship of men to himself. Demons are worshipped behind many of the images people tattoo on their bodies or pictures people put up in their homes. Satan uses people, places, and things to draw men into the worship of himself. When a believer worships God, he sends a message to every demon and to Satan himself of who the great one really is! Whether you worship in a church or at home, the greatest act of service to God you can render is to praise him, worship him, or to give thanks to his holy name.

Worship Is Acknowledging Lordship

There is so much more to be taught about worship than what can be put into one short chapter. However, I want to show you how your worship impacts your relationship with God. When you become a worshipper, you enter into an "intimate relationship" with the Lord. This intimacy gives you special consideration with the Lord. The Lord loves us all his children, but he does have favorites. His favorites are those who worship him. When a believer becomes a worshipper, he has favor with God. Let us consider a passage of scripture that is commonly read, but one point is often overlooked. "When he was come down from the mountain, great multitudes followed him" (Matthew 8:1). There were many people who followed Jesus because they had needs. But the Holy Spirit inspired the scripture writers to show us those persons who stood out with Lord. There was a large multitude of people, but then there was this one leper. "And behold, there came a leper and worshipped him, saying, Lord if thou wilt, thou can make me clean. And Jesus put forth his hand, and touched him, saying I will; be thou clean" (Matthew 8:2–3). The first thing that we should notice is that this leper "worshipped him." Notice that Jesus did not stop him from worshipping. There are many false teachers who will tell you, "Don't worship Jesus…worship God." But they, too, will bow down before the Lord Jesus Christ and worship him one day. Those who worshipped Jesus receive special favor with the Father. It was the leper's worship that made him stand out from the crowd. Next, we need to notice that the leper did not call Jesus teacher or master like the Pharisees. Instead, he called him Lord. Those who embrace lordship embrace worship because they know the worth of their Lord. Are you in the crowd of people who follow Jesus out of need, or have you become a worshipper?

Let us look at another instance of someone who gained favor with the Lord through their worship. In Matthew chapter 15, there is the story of the Syrophenician (Canaanite) woman.

> Then Jesus went thence, and departed into the coast of Tyre and Sidon. And behold, a woman of Canaan came out of the same coasts, and cried unto him, saying, 'Have mercy on me, O Lord, thou son of David: my daughter is grievously vexed with a devil.' But he answered her not a word. And his disciples came and besought him, saying, Send her away; for she crieth after us. (Matthew 15:21–23)

Here, we have a woman who had come to Jesus, and he would not so much as even talk to her. However, Jesus explained himself to his disciples so that they, and we, would have an understanding of why he was not talking to the woman. Jesus said to the disciples, "I am not sent but unto the lost sheep of the house of Israel" (Matthew 15:24). Jesus knew his assignment was to Israel. This meant that this lady did not yet qualify for this blessing of deliverance. She was not of the house of Israel, and Jesus had not yet died on the cross. However, the woman did something that many modern believers do not do. "Then came she and worshipped him, saying, Lord, help me" (Matthew 15:25). She does the exact same two things the leper did. She worshipped Jesus, and she called him Lord. When she did this, the same Jesus who would not so much as talk to her began to speak with her. "But he answered and said, It is not meet to take the children's bread, and cast it to the dogs." By this, Jesus was saying, "The blessings of God belong to the children of God." We can better understand Jesus's disposition with this analogy: If your daughter was on her way home from school, would you take her dinner and feed the dog with it? This Canaanite woman then said to Jesus, "True Lord; yet the dogs eat of the crumbs which fall from their masters table" (Matthew 15:27). By this, the woman acknowledges that she does not deserve this blessing, but in so many words, she is saying that it is a small thing (crumbs) for the Lord to deliver her daughter. Even the animals who are "in the master's house" eat some of the crumbs of food that fall from the table. By saying this, the Canaanite woman, by faith, puts herself into the family of God. She is asserting that the dog in the master's house is a part of the family! This woman's faith was relentless. "Then Jesus answered and said unto her, O woman, great is thy faith: be it unto thee even as thou wilt. And her daughter was made whole from that very hour" (Matthew 15:28). There is no doubt that this is a story of faith. However, if you only see faith, you will have missed so many other very important points. You should see that this woman's worship opened the door for the Lord to speak to her. You should also see that she saw him as her Lord. These two things are imperative if you are to walk in a lordship relationship.

"At His Feet"

Many people do not understand or perceive the relationship between the Lord Jesus and worship. All throughout his earthly ministry, Jesus healed the sick, raised the dead, and did many miracles. Those people who perceived his deity worshipped him. These scriptural acts of worship were often indicated by three small words, *at his feet*. At the feet of the Lord Jesus is where worship takes place. Falling down at the Lord's feet in worship is how many people get their breakthrough. After his resurrection, Jesus appeared to the women who came to the tomb. Matthew 28:9 says, "And as they went to tell his disciples, behold, Jesus met them saying 'all hail.' And they came and **held him by the feet, and worshipped him** (emphasis added)." Consider also Jairus's efforts to seek help for his daughter. "And behold, there cometh one of the rulers of the synagogue, Jairus by name; and when he saw him he **fell at his feet** (emphasis added). And besought him greatly, saying, 'My little daughter lieth to the point of death" (Mark 5:22–23). Because of Jairus's worship, his daughter was healed. But what about the woman with the alabaster box of ointment in the book of Luke? Did she worship?

> And one of the Pharisees desired him that he would eat with him, and he went into the Pharisee's house, and sat down to meat. And behold a woman of the city, which was a sinner, when she heard that Jesus sat at meat in the Pharisees house, brought and alabaster box of ointment, and stood **at his feet** behind weeping and began to **wash his feet with her tears**, and did wipe them with the hairs of her head, and **kissed his feet,** and anointed them with the ointment. (Luke 7:36–38, emphasis added)

This woman was worshipping at Jesus's feet. Consequently, without her asking, Jesus forgave her sins. "Her sins, which are many, are forgiven" (Luke 7:47). I have already mentioned the story of the ten lepers and how they got healed. Let us once again consider the one leper who got more than just healing. "And it came to pass that as they went, they were cleansed. And one of them, when he saw that he that he was healed, turned back and with a loud voice glorified God, and fell down on his face **at his feet**, giving him thanks" (Luke 17:14–16, emphasis added). It is important to note that men are not to be worshipped, but God is to be worshipped. Consider Peter in Acts chapter 10. "And as Peter was coming in, Cornelius met him, and **fell down at his feet and worshipped him.** But Peter took him up, saying, Stand up! I myself also am a man" (Acts 10:25–26, emphasis added). Notice that Jesus did not stop anyone from worshipping him, but Peter did. Revelation 5:12 says, "Worthy is the Lamb that was slain to receive power, and riches, and wisdom, and strength and honor, and glory and blessing." How is your relationship to the Lord Jesus? If it is not what you would want it to be, you can begin by the practice of worship. Those who worship the Lord receive from the Lord. The best place any man can be is *at the feet of the Lord*!

CHAPTER 10

Judgment of the Lord

It is said that the greatest fear of man is the idea that there is a supreme being somewhere in the universe who has the right to judge him. There is someone who can and will judge us. Every believer needs to have a revelation of Christ Jesus as judge. Every believer must also have a revelation of Christ not only as judge in a general sense but specifically as a personal judge. While some people may not like the idea of being judged, in reality, all our lives we are being judged. Our judgments begin as children in the home. When your mother said, "Bring me my belt!" she was judging you. Your work performance is judged by your boss. The police officer judges your driving. The instructor judges your learning. Then there are actual legal judges to rule on any criminal or civil matters you may be involved in. You can't even play sports without having officials there to judge the game. All of our lives we are being judged because judgment is a principle established by God, and it is applicable to any being that has free will. Free will necessitates judgment. God established free will with Adam in the garden of Eden when he said, "But of the tree of the knowledge good and evil, thou shall not eat of it" (Genesis 2:17). Once free will was established, there was the immediate need for consequences for Adam's choices and actions. In the same verse, God said to Adam, "For in the day that thou eat thereof, thou shall surely die" (Genesis 2:17). As long as we are in these imperfect bodies, we will be assisted by judges. The disposition to despise rules and judgment comes from the enemy and represents rebellion against God. God is the author of all judgment. He created it. He is the eternal judge. Lordship is living each day knowing that after you die, there will proceed your judgment. "It is appointed unto men once to die, but after this the judgment" (Hebrews 9:27). Living with this lordship awareness helps the believer to not take his choices and actions for granted. Judgment causes us to live our lives circumspectly.

Temporal Judge

God is the eternal judge. This means that after you die, he will decide your final and eternal state. But let us first consider the matter of temporal judgment. A temporal judgment is any judgment that is issued against you in this life. Temporal judgments are brought on by errors in our behavior or unrighteousness in our living. A temporal judgment can be as severe as God issuing the premature death of an individual. Even in the instance of death, the word *temporal* denotes the fact that God is judging the person for his immediate transgression, but it does not represent that individual's final judgment. The purpose of all temporal judgment is to correct something that is wrong about you. Another parallel phrase that is often used in connection with temporal judgment is *corrective action*. God issues temporal judgments often as a corrective measure. He is a Father, and he gives correction to his children according to his standards of righteousness. If the believer disregards Christ's lordship, he will eventually see the intervention of God's corrective judgment. Hebrews 12:7–8 says, "If ye endure chastisement, God deals with you as with sons. For what son is he whom the Father chastens not? But if ye be without chastisement, whereof all are partakers, then are ye bastards and not sons." I happen to work as a chaplain in a prison. The department that governs the prisons is called the Department of Corrections. The prison consists of many men and women who have stood before an earthly judge of law and have been convicted of a crime. These persons are sent to a correctional facility because there is something in their lives that needs correction. God is the author of all judgment. The police and criminal justice system are ordained of God to issue temporal judgments against men. God himself also issues temporal judgments on men. Lordship is knowing that we are subject to the Lord's temporal judgments, just was we will be subject to the Lord's eternal judgment.

There are many scriptures that speak of the intervention of God in the lives of believers through temporal judgments. Colossians 3:6 is speaking of sexual immorality in the believer. It references God issuing temporal judgment on believers when it says, "For which things sake the wrath of God cometh on the children of disobedience." The phrase *children of disobedience* is interpreted as those who are believers but have failed to live up to God's standards. Similarly, 1 Corinthians chapter 11 teaches us about Communion. The Lord expects that we as believers would show respect and reverence for the Holy Communion. It is the symbol of Jesus's body and his blood. Many of the believers in Corinth that this letter was written to did not show proper regard for the Holy Communion. First Corinthians 11:29–30 says, "For he that eateth and drinketh unworthily, eateth and drinketh damnation to himself, not discerning the Lord's body. For this cause, many are weak and sickly among you, and many sleep." Here we see that the Lord's hand was against those who did not show respect for the Holy Communion. The reference to "many sleep" means that some in the church had already died for their irreverence. In Acts chapter 5, we see Ananias and Sapphira come under the temporal judgment of the Lord for not giving the Holy Spirit his proper regard. There are some Christians who will declare that these types of temporal judgments were under the old covenant. However, all the scriptures I have mentioned here are New Testament scriptures. Before the Lord issues a temporal judgment against a believer, he will give him a chance to repent. Many believers I have met in the correctional facility have testified, "The Lord kept telling me to stop doing the things I was doing." If we do not live our lives under the lordship of Christ, we will be subject to the Lord's temporal judgment.

I have seen God judge believers for irreverence, for immorality, and even for their pride. These are not the only things God will judge the believer for, but they are certainly three that I have seen in my lifetime. I would also add that I have been on the receiving end of the wrath of God also. Many men have been judged by God for misusing the Lord's church. The church is not a place for sexual immorality, thievery, or pride. Pastors who do not walk reverently are dealt with by the Lord. A certain pastor was rejected by his congregation as immoral and told he would no longer be the pastor. He decided to take advantage of the situation and steal the church's resources. He took money, furniture, and supplies from the church and moved to another state. When he arrived in his new residence, he felt a bit sick. He scheduled an appointment to see a doctor on the next day. The doctor said, "You have advanced cancer. You do not have long to live. Have you not had any symptoms prior to this?" The pastor said, "No, I have always had excellent health." The pastor died a few weeks later. Excellent health will not help you when you are under the judgment of God. Situations like these happen often in our world. Many believers have come under the judgment of the Lord for unrighteous living. No amount of eloquent funeral speeches will change the reality that if our lives do not please God, we will lose our health, money, relationships, and even years off of our lives.

> Furthermore, we have had fathers of our flesh which corrected us and we gave them reverence: shall we not much rather be in subjection unto the Father of spirits and live. For they verily for a few days chastened us after their own pleasure: but he for our profit, that we might be partakers of his holiness. Now no chastisement for the present seems to be joyous, but grievous, nevertheless afterward it yields the peaceable fruit of righteousness unto them which are exercised thereby. (Hebrews 12:9–11)

There are Christian ministers who believe and teach that anything adverse that happens to a believer is not of God. Their theological premise is that God is a loving Father, and he would not consign any negative experience to his children. They believe that anything adverse that happens to a believer is of the devil. They make great efforts to defend the character of God. They believe that if they exclude God from anything that would seem like a judgment, then they are encouraging the believer's faith. However, we must remember that even an earthy father issues out judgments on his children, and the purpose of that judgment is love. There is a judgment that is meted out of love. Our heavenly Father does not contrive evil against his children; his deeds are always acts of righteousness. If our ways are wayward, then the Father is obliged to correct us. When the enemy strikes us, there is no love involved; but when God chastens us, it is for the purpose of correction. There is a difference between an attack and a chastisement although they may sometimes look the same. The need to make God innocent of all negative experiences in our lives is errant theology. There are believers who have spent months in the hospital because they would not submit to lordship. There are believers who have lost their marriages because they would not change their ways. There are believers who lost their jobs because of their disobedience. There are many chastisements that are not at the level of someone dying. Many ministers' misguided defense of God's character actually becomes a defense against accountability to Christ. The Holy Spirit in the believer will allow him to discern the difference between an attack of the enemy and a chastisement from the Lord.

In 2 Samuel chapter 11, David committed adultery with a married woman whose name was Bathsheba. David took Bathsheba into his home, had her husband Uriah killed, and made her his wife. For a period of approximately two years, David had gotten away with these egregious acts. After God had given him time to repent and David had not repented, God stepped in to judge David. The judgment from God was that David was to die for what he had done. God sent the prophet Nathan to him for one last opportunity for David to recognize the error of his ways. Nathan shared with David the story of a man who had one lamb in which he loved, and there came a rich man who took the man's one and only lamb (2 Samuel 12:1–5). After hearing the story, David's anger was kindled. He declared to Nathan that whoever this rich man was who had taken the man's one and only lamb would surely die (2 Samuel 12:5). From David's own mouth, he pronounced his judgment! Nathan said to David, "Thou art the man" (2 Samuel 12:7). David subsequently repents of the things he had done. He declared, "I have sinned against the Lord!" (2 Samuel 12:13) This repentance gave God, the judge, room to show David mercy. Nathan declared, "The Lord also has put away thy sins; thou shalt not die." But God's mercy to David would not prevent corrective discipline against David. Nathan said, "The child also that is born unto thee shall surely die" (2 Samuel 12:14). This was a judgment from the Lord. The text says that the child that Uriah's wife bore unto David was suddenly very sick (2 Samuel 12:15). There is no mention that the devil made the child sick, because it was a judgment from the Lord. There is no need for us to defend the Lord. David's intervention for his son through intercessory prayer and fasting would not change the judge's decision. David's son died (2 Samuel 12:18).

The Dispensation of Grace

The temporal judgments of the Lord are all throughout the scripture. We tend to speak and act as if there are no judgments under the dispensation of grace. We like to teach that the blood of Jesus appeased the wrath of God and there is only God's mercy and grace for us today. But God's mercy and grace are applicable only when the believer is in submission to Christ's lordship. These statements about mercy and grace are true when reverently applied. Jesus's blood has appeased the wrath of God. The Lord has mercy for those who will receive his mercy respectfully. However, for those who will not have God's mercy, they will have his wrath. Let us investigate another New Testament scripture where the apostle Peter talks about God issuing temporal judgments in the past.

> Whose judgment now of a long time lingers not,
> and their damnation slumbers not. For if God
> spared not the angels that sinned, but cast them
> down to hell, and delivered them into chains
> of darkness, to be reserved unto judgment; and

> spared not the old world, but saved Noah the
> eighth person, a preacher of righteousness, bring-
> ing in the flood upon the world of the ungodly;
> and turning the cities of Sodom and Gomorrah
> into ashes condemned them with and overthrow,
> making them and example unto those that after
> should live ungodly. And delivered just Lot, vexed
> with the filthy conversation of the wicked…
> The Lord knows how to deliver the godly out of
> temptations, and to reserve the unjust unto the
> Day of Judgment to be punished. (2 Peter 2:3–9)

In the scripture above, Apostle Peter expounds upon the future fate of the enemies of God's people. He assures the believers that their enemies would be judged by God even though that judgment had for a lone time lingered. Peter cites three different instances of God's temporal judgments in history: (1) God judged the rebellion of Lucifer and the fallen angels, casting them out of heaven, (2) God judged the wickedness that was on the earth during Noah's day by sending the great flood, and (3) God judged Sodom and Gomorrah, bringing that city to ashes and making an example of it. With these historical records of God's temporal judgments, Peter assures the believers that God was faithful to judge those who were now persecuting them. Apostle Peter reminds them and us that God has not abandoned his status as judge. There is still to come a future day of judgment and punishment. There are things that have been consigned to the future day of judgment so that we can enjoy grace and mercy today. However, the grace and mercy you are experiencing today will not prevent God's judgment of the unrighteousness tomorrow.

Eternal Judgment: The Judgment Seat of Christ

Eternal judgment is the final judgment from God that you will receive after you die and leave this world. It is fearful to think that we will be judged by God in this way. Second Corinthians 5:10–11 says, "For we must all appear before the judgment seat of Christ; that everyone may receive the things done in his body, according to that he hath done, whether it be good or bad. Knowing then the terror of the Lord, we persuade men." Eternal judgment will be that great day and place where God will set all things right at his mighty judgment seat. At the eternal judgment, everything that has been done wrong will be made right. On that day, every person who was secretly injured, hurt, or killed by someone will be avenged. On that day, men will be rewarded for the good things that they have done, even things that no one knew about. On that day, men will be punished for the sins they have committed and kept concealed. Many things in our world have gone unjudged, but it has not gone unnoticed. Many people today spend too much time griping about "this is not right" and "that is not right." They get disheartened about the imperfections of man and the imperfections in this world. But the answer is not in man. Judgment day will bring divine justice to every wayward situation, and God will set right every wrong.

On judgment day, who will do the judging? John 5:22–23 says, "For the Father judges no man, but hath committed all judgment unto the Son: That all men should honor the Son, even as they honor the Father." All men will stand before Jesus Christ in judgment. There is no other Judge. "The Father judges no man." The same men who have denied, minimized, blasphemed, and denounced Jesus will stand before him to receive their final judgment. At our judgment, everything we have ever done will be in review. Ecclesiastes 12:14 says, "For God shall bring every work into judgment, with every secret thing, whether it be good, or whether it be evil." Our Lord Jesus has also said, "But I say unto you, That every idle word that men shall speak, they shall give account thereof in the day of judgment" (Matthew 12:36). When a believer knows he will stand before God one day, it gives him the motivation to be diligent to live the life that God has called him to live. Modern men resist even the thought of God's judgment. They prefer to believe that judgment does not apply. God remains judge even when men refuse to accept it. Acts 17:31 says, "Because he [God] hath appointed a day in which he will judge the world in righteousness by that man whom he hath ordained; whereof he hath given assurance unto all men, in that he hath raised him from the dead."

The Great White Throne Judgment

And I saw a great white throne, and him that sat on it, from whose face the earth and the heaven fled away; and there was found no place for them. And I saw the dead, small and great, stand before God; and the books were opened: and another book was opened which is the book of life: and the dead were judged out of those things which were written in the books, according to their works. And the sea gave up the dead which were in it; and death and hell delivered up the dead which were in them: and they were judged every man according to their works. And death and hell were cast into the Lake of fire. This is the second death. And whosoever was not found written in the book of life was cast into the lake of fire. (Revelation 20:11–15)

I have talked about the judgment of the believer because believers are the focus of this book. However, the Bible is explicitly clear concerning the judgment of the unbeliever. All men will be judged. Revelation chapter 20 gives us a picture of the judgment of the nations. There are many people who have lived, but they did not know of Christ or were never exposed to the gospel. The judgment scene in Revelation chapter 20 is characterized by the opening of "books." God has recorded all of the acts and works of the unbeliever. When these men stand before God's great judgment seat, the Lord will open the Books of Works. At this great judgment, every man will have to recall everything he has ever done. He will be judged by God based on his choices and actions. The above scripture declares that death, hell, and the sea will deliver up all the souls that are there. Those men and women who lived throughout the ages will stand before God and give an account of their living.

CHAPTER 11

The Reality of Hell

Testimony: On my way to hell—prophetic dream (June 26, 2021)

On June 26, 2021, I lay down to sleep on an ordinary Saturday night. Then suddenly, as I was sleeping, things changed. I could suddenly feel my spirit man beginning to separate from my body. It was separating just like someone would peel a piece of tape off a table. My spirit man was coming out of my body as I was actively dying. My thoughts were, *I am dying tonight!* Also, I became acutely aware that I was damned (consigned to punishment) to hell. Suddenly, I saw a black vortex that came up out of the earth, and it was positioned right beneath where I was lying. This black hole had the appearance of a tornado. It was a portal to hell. The black hole was hell reaching up to receive me. This black hole also had a strong vacuum to it. It was pulling at my spirit man even before it fully separated from my body. The strongest sensation I could feel was that I did not know Jesus, and this was the reason I was going to hell. I felt helpless. I could not stop what was happening to me. Thoughts ran through my head: *My wife will find me dead tomorrow morning. I can't believe I am leaving this earth so soon.* I could also sense that the greatest terrors, horrors, and pain awaited me there, down inside that portal. I could sense the presence of agony and great suffering that was inside that portal. Suddenly, I screamed in terror, and my spirit man reentered my body! My wife awoke and shook me. She said, "Mark, are you okay? That was the most blood-curling scream I have ever heard!" I began to tell her that I was actively dying and the things I had just experienced. I sought the Lord Jesus as to the meaning of that experience. The Lord showed me that he was allowing me to feel what people feel when they die without knowing the Lord. The Lord said to me, "People are dying and going to hell, and my people do not care! This is not my heart!" The moment you die, if you do not know the Lord Jesus, hell will open itself up to receive you. "He that hath the Son hath life: and he that hath not the Son of God hath not life." (1 John 5:12) Salvation is on the earth! Salvation is in the Lord Jesus Christ!

Lordship means believing that the Bible and more specifically the teachings of Jesus are our primary truth and the bases for our life. Jesus believed in both eternal judgment and hell and taught about them profusely. The believer who is under lordship believes the same, without variation. There are many people today who believe in annihilation. This is the belief that when a person dies, they will cease to exist. Many other people are hoping that annihilationism is a reality. If annihilationism is true, you can live your life any way you would like, and when you die, you will only cease to exist. That would be quite convenient for some people. But annihilationism is a lie. You are an eternal being, and you will continue to exist even after you die, in one place or another. The belief in heaven or hell as an after-death experience was a great focus of Jesus's ministry. It was so central to the teachings of our Lord that to exclude it would be tantamount to dismantling the faith. Any Christianity that does not include teaching on both heaven and hell is a false religion. One of the deceptions of the enemy is to cause people to disconnect from the reality of hell. When people are not taught about hell, salvation diminishes in its significance. Many Christian ministers today are telling people they need to be saved but not wanting to offend them by sharing with them what they need to be saved from. These ministers preach only about the earthly benefits of knowing the Lord. The result is carnal Christians who believe this earth is their heaven. A Christianity that is not predicated upon the reality of salvation from hellfire is an ineffective belief system. Any Christianity that does not embrace the reality of hell does not embrace the cross and does not glorify Christ Jesus. If you are not sharing with people that Jesus came to save us from hell and its fire, you are merely preaching humanism. The reality of eternal punishment should literally shutter in the hearts of men and women. The reality of hell will cause men to cling to the Lord. Men are saved not simply by knowing that Jesus died for our sins. Men are saved when they know that Jesus died to deliver us from hell.

In our modern culture, the reality of hell has been intentionally commercialized. We are bombarded with scary movies, television shows, Halloween parties, and video games that all have demonic images. Our culture has desensitized and conditioned men to accept ideas of hell and demons as "entertainment." This is the design of the enemy to cause modern man to not think about his eternal state. But when we listen to our Lord Jesus, we get a gravely different picture. Jesus said, "And fear not them which kill the body, but are not able to kill the soul: but rather fear him which is able to destroy both soul and body in hell" (Matthew 10:28). God not only can kill your body, but he will also decide the eternal disposition of your body and soul. Hell is a place of great torment. The idea that a person can spend eternity in a place of torment is difficult for the modern-day pleasure-seeker to imagine. But that does not make hell any less real. John 3:16 is one of the most popular and beloved scriptures in the Bible. Even John 3:16 references the fact that God sent Jesus to prevent us from perishing. "For God so loved the world, that he gave his only begotten son, that whosoever believes in him should not perish but have everlasting life" (John 3:16). The word *perish* is not referencing physical death. If it did mean physical death, no one who believes in Jesus would die physically. This reference is instead referring to a deeper sense of "perishing" than a physical death. It is referencing perishing in hell. Hell was not intended originally for man. It was created for the devil and the fallen angels. Speaking of future judgment, Jesus says that at their judgment, some men will hear these words: "Depart from me, ye cursed, into everlasting fire, prepared for the devil and his angels" (Matthew 25:41). Hell is the punishment place of the devil and the fallen angels. However, as a result of the fall of Adam, men have been separated from God. Men are now born with a sinful nature. Consequently, mortal men will share the same eternal punishment as the devil if they are not redeemed to God. God has graciously offered man a lifeline of salvation from eternal punishment in the cross of our Lord Jesus Christ. Through the shedding of the blood of Jesus and his subsequent death on the cross, men can avoid ever having to experience hell. This is no laughing matter, and hell is nothing to take lightly. In fact, you should devote your entire life to avoiding it!

Where is hell? The Bible suggests that hell is underneath us, at the center of the earth. Job 17:16 says, "They shall go down to the bars of the pit, when our rest together is in the dust." The punishments men will endure in hell are permanent and eternal. Jesus said, "And if thy hand offend thee, cut it off: it is better for thee to enter into life maimed, than having two hands to go into hell, into the fire that never shall be quenched: Where their worm dieth not, and the fire is not quenched" (Mark 9:43–44). Teaching about hell was a priority of Jesus, and it should be a priority for all believers. How often do you hear sermons about hell? Jesus himself was not exempt from experiencing hell. A part of his coming down to earth from heaven to bring salvation to man was that he would go into hell. Acts 2:27 references the prophecies of David who was speaking of the Lord Jesus, saying, "Because thou wilt not leave my soul in hell, neither wilt thou suffer thine Holy One to see corruption." Many people often say that "a loving God will not send someone to a place of eternal torment!" God sent Jesus to that place. If Jesus was required to go to hell to save men from their sins, what man will subsequently say that he can reject the Savior and still be exempt from going to hell? We tend to believe in polar opposites. We believe that there is hot and cold, summer and winter, and night and day. So if there is a heaven, why would there not be a hell? Many people are so bound to this world that in their "shortsightedness" they do not see what is coming. This world will end, and this earth as we know it will one day dissolve. You cannot live for this world nor for the things in it. "But the day of the Lord will come as a thief in the night; in the which the heavens shall pass away with a great noise, and the elements shall melt with fervent heat, the earth also and the works that are therein shall be burned up (2 Peter 3:10). How foolish it is for someone to live for the things in this temporary world. The reality of hell should burn in the hearts and minds of every believer.

The Rich Man and Lazarus

"For I am tormented in this flame!" (Luke 16:24)

In Luke 16:19–31, Jesus tells a story of a rich man who had great material wealth and an impoverished beggar named Lazarus who sat daily outside the rich man's gate. This story is told by Jesus to give us insight into the reality and revelation of hell. We are told in the story that this poor beggar named Lazarus "desired to be fed with the crumbs from the rich man's table" (Luke 16:21). When you listen to the story, it initially seems like a referendum on the rich man's failure to have generosity. However, it would seem that the more salient point of the story would instead be that status and accomplishments in this world are impertinent to whether a person goes to heaven or to hell. The wealth and status of the rich man does not prevent him from going to hell. The next part of the story informs us that the angels are involved in harvesting the souls of those who die belonging to the Lord. It is interesting to note that the angels are directly involved in the death of the beggar but conspicuously absent in the death of the rich man. "The beggar died and was carried by the angels into Abraham's bosom: the rich man also died and was buried." But the thing we should pay even closer attention to is how this story gives us insights into what hell is really like. We are told that the rich man's body was buried. Yet we are also told that "in hell he lifted up his eyes" (Luke 16:23). This apprises us that those in hell will still have a body. We are also told explicitly that the rich man was in torment (Luke 16:23). This rich man cried out for mercy, begging for even a drop of water (Luke 16:24). Many people have romanticized hell, minimizing the reality of it. We should, however, carefully consider the words of this rich man. He tells us unequivocally that he is tormented by the fire. "For I am in torment in this flame" (Luke 16:24). This story is told by the Lord Jesus as a warning to us all. It is not figurative. It is not symbolic. It is literal! While in hell, this rich man still retained his memory. He remembered his father's house and all his brothers who were still alive back on earth. He begged for someone to return to earth to warn his family about the reality of hell. "I pray thee therefore father that thou would send him to my father's house: for I have five brethren; that he may testify unto them, lest they also come into this place of torment" (Luke 16:27–28). In hell, you will be tormented by the fire. You will be tormented by the regret of your choices. You will be tormented by the fear that your loved ones may end up in the same condition as yourself. Also, those who enter hell are tormented by the fact that they have missed out on heaven because they refused to accept and submit to the Lord Jesus Christ.

The Sign of Jonah

> An evil and adulterous generation seeketh after a
> sign; and there shall no sign be given to it, but the
> sign of the prophet Jonah. For as Jonah was three
> days and three nights in the whale's belly; so shall
> the Son of man be three days and three nights in
> the heart of the earth. (Matthew 12:39–40)

In the above reference, Jesus was talking with the scribes and Pharisees when they requested of him a sign. It had become widely known that Jesus would often perform miracles. One of them said to Jesus, "Master, we would see a sign from thee" (Matthew 12:38). By making this request, they were affectively saying, "Do a miracle so that we can believe in you." They were asking Jesus for proof that he was sent from God. Jesus retorted that the only "sign" they would be given would be the sign of his impending death, burial, and resurrection, which had already been symbolized in the life of the prophet Jonah. With these words, Jesus implicates that the story of Jonah and the whale is both symbolic of hell and revelational of himself. Every believer should be sure to understand that the work our Lord had to complete included (1) teaching men the ways of God, (2) offering himself on the cross as a sacrifice and propitiation for our sins, and (3) spending an abbreviated length of time in hell as substitutionary punishment on our behalf. Any believer who does not understand these things is missing the essentials. In fact, salvation is predicated upon you believing that Jonah spent three days and three nights in the belly of a whale and that Jesus likewise spent three days and nights in the heart of the earth. Jesus went to hell so that you and I won't have to go there. But just as the whale spit out Jonah alive, so did God raise Jesus from the dead and brought him forth out of the pit of hell!

If we read the text of Jonah chapters 1 and 2 carefully, we can clearly see that two things happened to Jonah. Firstly, he was swallowed up by the giant fish. "And the Lord had prepared a great fish to swallow up Jonah. And Jonah was in the belly of the fish three days and three nights" (Jonah 1:17). Also, Jonah 2:1 tells us that Jonah prayed to the Lord while he was in the fish's belly. "Then Jonah prayed unto the Lord his God out of the fish's belly." However, a close reading of the text would cause us to conclude that Jonah died while he was in the fish's belly. I say this because the expressions of Jonah move from the fish as the focus, to actually speaking of being in hell. "I went down to the bottoms of the mountains: the earth with her bars was about me forever: yet hast thou brought up my life from corruption, O Lord my God" (Jonah 2:6). The word *corruption* references the potential rotting of the body after a person has been dead for so many days. There is a parallel expression concerning corruption that is speaking of the Lord Jesus. Psalm 16:10 is speaking of Jesus's death. It says, "For thou will not leave my soul in hell; neither will thou suffer thine Holy One to see corruption." Again, it is my belief that Jonah died and went to hell while in the whale's belly. You may disagree. It is not mandatory for salvation. It is just my personal conclusion. Perhaps the best witness I can share on this matter is Jonah's own testimony. "I cried by reason of mine affliction unto the Lord, and he heard me; out of the belly of hell cried I, and thou heardest my voice." Many scholars believe that Jonah is referencing his "afflictions" while in the whale's belly. I happen to believe that Jonah, being a type of Christ, was both swallowed by the whale, then died and went into hell. If Jonah is a type of Christ, we know that one of the essential tenets of the Christian faith is resurrection. Jonah had to be brought back to life as a type of resurrected person. Jonah 2:10 says, "And the Lord spake unto the fish, and it vomited out Jonah upon the dry land." If a large fish had to vomit, it probably would vomit right there in the water. But this fish knew that the instruction of the Lord was to put the package back onto the dry land. The Lord Jesus came to reverse all the damnation that was appointed to us by Adam's fall. If the Lord Jesus had to go to hell for the punishment of our sins, how can those who reject him believe they will not go there?

Testimony #2: Table of torment—prophetic dream: February 28, 2022

On the night of February 28, 2022, I was asleep in my bed. I don't know how long I had been asleep; God knows. As I slept, a portal to hell was opened to me. Suddenly, I was in a completely different realm. I was in hell. There in hell, I was strapped to a table of torment. I felt a deep sense of acute fear and hopelessness. It was a hopelessness so profound that it felt like I had been abandoned by God. There was a large demon standing over me. He was wearing a black robe. His arm was extended across my body. I could see his hand as it extended from the sleeves of the black robe. It was a bony hand, almost skeletal-like, but it had some type of skin on it. I could not see his face, as I was strapped down on a table, and he was standing near my head. I could hear him speak. He said, "The first time you experienced hell, you got away, but I got you now!" I lifted my head from the table, and there was a tunnel of molten lava burning at my feet. In fact, the intense heat of the lava was the only light in the room. I was about to be physically inserted into the lava. The reality of being strapped to a table and seeing the lava was beyond horrific. The experience was very dynamic and beyond overwhelming! The fear you experience in hell is far beyond the fear that one experiences on earth. The fear in hell is many times more intense. I cannot describe the intensity of the fear. We often use the phrase "I was terrified," but that does not grasp the intensity of the fear in hell. Your worst earthly fear is tolerable compared to the fears of hell. If you could capture the fear that you would experience if you were about to be thrown over the edge of a mountain cliff or the fear you would have if you were about to be thrown to hungry lions or the fear you would have if you were about to be run over by a large truck going ninety miles an hour, it would not commensurate the fear of the tortures of hell. The fears of hell are many more times the intensity of fear on earth. The fear is so intense that it is actually painful; and it is a part of the torment of hell. There is no peace in hell. There is no love in hell. There is no joy in hell. There is no rest in hell. There is only torment. Suddenly, by the grace of the Lord, I began to be able to pull out of that realm and come back to this one. As I began to pull out of the vision, I could still see hell, but I began to simultaneously be able to see the periphery of my bedroom. As I continued to pull out of it more, I could see more of my bedroom, but I could also still see the demon and the table of torment. I kept leaving that realm and returning to the earth until finally, I was completely back in my bedroom wide awake.

Mercy Is on the Earth

In these latter days, the Lord Jesus is giving many more believers witness of hell through visions and visitation experiences. There are many people in our world today who deny the existence of hell. There are others who actively repress the thoughts of it. However, these denials of its existence will not change its realities, nor will it distort its purpose. Jesus is the only one who can save a man from hell. The Bible says, "He that believes on the Son hath everlasting life: and he that believes not the Son shall not see life; but the wrath of God abides on him" (John 3:36). When one is in hell, there is no more chance for him to obtain mercy. There is no more place for repentance. Mercy is on the earth. You must cry out to God and ask Jesus Christ to save you while you are still here on this earth, for there will be no mercy for you in hell. The ministers of God must stir themselves up to tell this generation the truth about hell. When believers cease to be taught about hell, they consequently stop being thankful for the work Jesus did for them on the cross. Calvary's cross is the center of the Christian faith. However, man will be grateful for that salvation only when he knows that judgment is inevitable. This generation of believers feel entitled to salvation instead of being deeply grateful for the Lord Jesus's work on the cross. We are to spend our lives reverently thanking the Lord for his suffering, for his work, and for our salvation—from hell!

End

ABOUT THE AUTHOR

Mark D. Michael is a chaplain and writer. He holds a doctor of ministry degree from United Seminary in Dayton, Ohio. He has served in ministry for over thirty years. He has served as a hospital chaplain for the Veterans Administration and as a local pastor. He currently serves as a correctional chaplain for the Alabama Department of Corrections, working from Kilby Correctional Facility in Montgomery, Alabama. He and his wife, Sandra, live in Union Springs, Alabama. Mark is also the author of the book *False Adequacy*.